Personal Wealth

How to Save, Track, and Grow Your Money,

To Achieve

Financial Security, Independence, and Wealth

By Larry E. Craig

2016

Second Edition

All Feedback Welcomed, E-mail:

LCraig1016@SBCGlobal.Net

Table of Contents

Acknowledgements 5

Introduction 7

Chapter 1   What Am I on This Earth To

Accomplish? 13

Chapter 2   The Light Bulb Goes On! 18

Chapter 3   What is Financial Security? . . 28

Chapter 4   Where Do I Save 49

Chapter 5   Financial Independence, Retirement, and Wealth 55

Chapter 6   How Do I Get a 6% Return?. . 65

Chapter 7   Earning Income 78

Chapter 8   Spending 91

Chapter 9   Time 110

Chapter 10   Action 114

Index

The List of Larry's Rules 119

Larry's Recommended List of Index Funds and Mutual
Funds 122

Larry's Reading List 124

Acknowledgements

For many years I shared the information I read in several books on saving and investing money with my wife, Janeen. I told her that I wished the authors had included a lot of other information that I felt they missed. She suggested I write my own book. So, I did.

I want to thank her for not only giving me the nudge that got me started with this book, but for also helping me with editing and proof reading. She also has had some really good ideas over the years that I have adopted and they are now part of this book.

Introduction

We have a crisis in our country. It is a personal financial crisis that is for the most part self-created. Many people are living their entire adult lives without any net worth, or in many cases, just a negligible amount. Another way to say it is they have almost no savings, no substantial equity built up in a house, little or no stocks or bonds, or other financial instruments such as CD's, IRA's, etc.

We have an abundance of statics and studies that show us that the problem is wide spread. For instance, here are just a few items that I recently read in my local newspaper or on the Internet:

A. Half of U.S. households headed by a person 55 and over have stashed away very little, to no retirement savings. The data comes from a report published by the U.S. Government Accountability Office. They reported that 59% of people age 55 to 64 have some saving's, however the amounts are often very small. In this group, about half have accumulated $104,000 or less; 24% have $25,000 in savings or less.

B. Approximately 63% of Americans have no emergency savings for things such as a $1,000 emergency room visit or a $500 car repair, according to a survey released by personal finance website Bankrate.com. Faced with an emergency, they say they would raise the money by reducing spending elsewhere (23%), borrowing from family and/or friends (15%), or using credit cards to bridge the gap (15%). Bankrate also found that four in 10 Americans either experienced a major unexpected expense over the past 12 months or had an immediate family member who had an unexpected expense.

C. A U.S. Federal Reserve survey found that "Savings are depleted for many households after the recession of 2008-2009. Among those who had savings prior to 2008, 57% said they had used up some or all of their savings in the Great Recession and its aftermath".

D. A survey by GOBankingRates.com found that most Americans (62%) have less than $1,000 in their savings account (although that does not include retirement or other investment accounts).

E. Only 22% of workers are very confident that they will have enough money for a comfortable retirement according to the Employee Benefit Research Institute's 2015 Retirement Confidence Survey.

F. The percentage of workers age 75 and older is expected to almost double in 2024 to 10.6 percent from the 1994 rate of 5.4 percent according to estimates from the Bureau of Labor Statistics.

These are troubling statistics and they paint a picture of Americans in crisis. The focus of some of these articles is about people getting ready to retire. I want to emphasize that being financially secure is important at any age, and as we all know, a real dilemma for those who are near retirement. This is why I point out in this book that achieving financial security is one of the most satisfying and life changing accomplishments you will ever achieve for yourself and your family.

One of the questions I ask myself is why are so many people clueless about savings and wealth building? It appears to me they are taking their obsession to spend every penny to the extreme by living most of their adult lives on the edge of financial disaster. Since it is a subject that I consider myself and expert on, I talk about this subject with people all of the time, and here are a list of the top reasons, in my opinion, that so many people are basically broke.

1. A lot of people tell themselves they will start saving for retirement once they reach age 40 or 45, but when the time comes, they have a million excuses for not ever really getting started. Of course, starting that late to build net worth is a huge mistake anyway.
2. Many people just are incapable of thinking out further that a few weeks or a few months. They sometimes bounce around from one crisis to another, so there is never a good time to focus on long term goals.
3. Some people actually like living on the edge of disaster. It is a kind of thrill seeking lifestyle and a badge of honor. I have had people tell me that they know they will have to work until they are 80 years old. Their plan is they intend to live their retirement in the present and worry about being broke at retirement age when they get there.
4. More often, people just do not understand how you build financial security over a long period of time. In my opinion, it is a lack of education about this critical financial skill that holds them back.

5. In a lot of cases, it is just a lack of will and the discipline that goes with it. Especially for people who are un-willing to deny themselves the latest fashions, shoes, the hottest cars, a larger house, or really anything they want whether they can afford it or not. Their focus is on spending money now, and taking on debt is not given any thought. This is another variant of number 3.

6. Of course, there are issues that can interrupt plans to save, such as: Being laid off from work, career changes, divorces, re-marriage, health issues, etc. These are real problems but all too often, people never get back on-track building wealth.

So, this list of excuses and reasons for living a lifetime of insufficient wealth and savings brings up the next question. What is the best way to have a satisfying and sound financial life?

Reading this book is a good first step to changing whatever you are doing now and getting on track to achieving financial security. Educating yourself is always better than being in the dark. In addition, I have a list of other books to read in the index that compliment the knowledge you will have after reading my book.

Once you have the knowledge about what to do and how to do it, what else do you need? Really just 3 things are necessary to secure yourself financially: 1. a steady, dependable, average to above-average income. 2. The will and the discipline to make yourself follow your plan and put your financial success above all other goals and distractions. 3. Acceptance of the trade-off that you would rather live below your means now, so that in return, you can build and later have a big, fat bank account or brokerage account that nobody knows about but you. If you can do these 3 things, you will one day live the rest of your life in the contented state of knowing that whatever life throws at you, you have the financial where-with-all to handle it! After all, what could be more important in your life than being financially secure?

If you want even more for yourself, you could choose to move your wealth goal up a notch to the next level, from financial security to financial independence. It just takes a little more time and savings.

Building wealth is a long term goal, it will not happen overnight. As I have already mentioned, it is more about determination and discipline than how much money you make. However, how much you make is very important and I will give you my suggestion about career choices and changes that will help you increase your earning power. Most importantly, achieving financial security is not rocket science. It is a skill anyone can learn and put into practice.

I hope reading this book is the beginning of a life changing event for you. No one deserves it more than you.

Larry E. Craig

Chicago, 2016

Chapter 1

What Am I On This Earth To Accomplish?

I graduated from college with a degree in International Business, and my former wife had a degree in accounting and was a CPA. Yet, 7 short years after getting our degrees and starting our business careers, we sat down like we did every December to set goals for ourselves for the coming year. But this particular year there was just silence. You see, we had achieved the big goal we had set for ourselves over the course of that year, which was to buy a custom made, large house in a new, upper middle class neighborhood. It was our third house and we put a lot of time and energy into making that house a reality.

So here we sat looking at each other in silence, having reached the one and only financial goal we both agreed on, and as far as the future was concerned for us, we both drew a blank. Now you need to take into consideration we were both still not even 30 years old yet! We were both hard working and dedicated to our jobs. We took a lot of satisfaction in helping our employers make more money and we were both skilled at finding solutions for their problems. I look back at that time and I am amazed that with all the schooling we had, and with the variety and depth of experience we had in the business world, and still, we did not have a clue as to what was the next goal for us to put on our plate. We had no philosophy or insight about what we wanted to achieve in life other than getting another raise and a promotion so we could make more money!

Like many of you, I came from a hard working middle class family. Many problems were hidden from me as a child, yet there was enough money so that I got most of whatever I wanted, including a college education. But here is a key part: my parents never talked to me about money, never trained me on how to budget, or balance a check book, or even discussed what goals they had for themselves. I think my Great Depression, World War II parents wanted to shield me to some extent from the worry and pain they had experienced concerning a lack of money in their childhood. I also think they felt you just figure things out for yourself when the time comes.

Like many families today, I don't think my parents even had mutual financial goals. They pretty much just made it week to week and month to month, and the years just clipped on by. Any long term savings came from a corporate thrift plan they participated in at work, and my father had a pension to rely on when they retired.

However, I want to make it clear that I am not blaming my parents for my lack of financial insight. In addition to growing up with a lot of love, I learned important lessons from my parents that served me well as I began my adult life. I learned good values from them just by watching what they did, even if there was not a lot of conversation about money. They did come together to save for new cars, a kitchen makeover, or for a family vacation. And they were frugal and knew how to stretch a dollar. Also, my parents bought a nice middle class home that they paid for by the time they retired. I am sure they brought me up in much the same way they were raised, and with the same silence about money and life goals they encountered in their childhood.

At college, I was trained on how to serve my employer. I discussed and practiced on how to make them more successful, on how to reduce their taxes, and how to increase their sales and profits. My college did a good job. I hit the ground running right after school and my college educations prepared me for what I encountered as soon as I got situated on the job. However, I can tell you that after 5 years in the business world it began to grate on me that I spent so much of my waking hours on bettering the life and finances of someone else, and at the expense of not focusing on my own life. That feeling began to well-up in me to a point that I knew I had to do something different or my life's work was going to be about making someone else rich and comfortable while my life just rambled on without real direction.

So not at home and not at school did I get the knowledge and insight I needed to learn about how to increase my wealth and how to make myself financially secure. Really the only thing I knew or talked about was just to go out and make as much money as you can, and that is what I did.

I am sure a lot of you have had a similar experience like mine. An almost total void of learning about financial issues at home, or maybe even worse, you learned the wrong things to do. Either way, you entered the adult world totally unprepared to navigate your way to a successful financial life. You were set up for a life of possible financial failure or at best, a mediocre financial life. Thankfully, I became aware of my shortcomings and I was determined to get the answers for myself. I went on to read and search for what information I could find. In my mid-thirties, I enrolled in courses that led to me becoming a Certified Financial Planner licensee. But most of all, I searched on my own to find out what to do and what to shot for, and that is what the rest of this book is about. I want to fill in the blanks for you on what you did not learn at home, or college, or help you get straight on what you were misled about concerning your financial life. The key point here is that not only do you need to know what to do, and in my mind that is the easiest part, but you also need to know the why, and the why is the hard part. Many people know what to do, at least in part, but they have not convinced themselves about why it is important until it is too late in life to do anything about it! So they treat their financial security as a low priority, as something I will do when I have the time, which means never.

As I go along, I will highlight and list **Larry's Rules**. These are my list of ideas that I feel you have to grasp and put into action in order to get what you want in life. Some or most of them you have probably heard before but I want you to know how my ideas fit together to form a financial philosophy that will backstop all of your financial decisions and thinking. And also give you the confidence about the direction your financial life is taking so that you can say no when you need to, and yes to moves that will make your life better.

I also want you to know that what I am about to pass on to you is not rocket science. In fact, it is the very simplicity of my message that I think you will find amazing. You see, we learn and hear so much now that everything just sometimes runs together leaving you grasping for what is important and what is not, and that creates a lot of doubt about what you need to do. The very essence of achieving wealth in your lifetime is sticking to a few deeply learned and understood truths and lessons, and then using them over and over again in your daily life.

Chapter 2

The Light Bulb Goes On!

If I asked you what your primary, lifetime financial goal is what would you say? Would you say to make a lot of money, or to retire comfortably at age 65? By the way, those are good goals, but they lack the philosophical understanding, the specificity, and the commitment to discipline that I think you have to have in order to make building wealth and financial security a focused part of your daily life.

So that leads me to my first Larry's Rule:

1. **Your lifetime, primary financial goal is to build net worth.**

I want you to repeat this rule over and over to yourself for a while until it is stuck in your mind. Now let me define what net worth is.

Take a pad of paper and write down in the form of a list, everything that you own. Assign a value to each item or category (such as clothes and shoes) that you feel is what it is worth today. Be conservative here, we are not talking about replacement value but what it would be worth if you had to sell it, or donate it to charity today. It is usually best to start your list with cash, or near cash items, such as cash in your bank account, savings, CD's, retirement accounts, investments, cash value of life insurance policies, etc., and then progress to clothes, furniture, cars, houses, china, boats, pianos, everything. Then add them all up, see exhibit 2.1.

On the next page list all of your debts with the remaining loan balance. Again, start with the most immediate you have to pay which is usually credit card debt, car loans, student loans, home equity loans, mortgage on your house, all debts that you owe. If you do not know what your loan balance is on a loan, go to the last year end-statement you received. Usually you can find it there but in some cases, you may have to call the lender and ask them to figure a loan payoff. Now add up all of your debt.

Next subtract the total of all of your debt from the total of all of your assets (the items you own). What is left over is your net worth on this day, month and year of your life. Here is the formula with some made up numbers:

Exhibit 2.1 Net Worth Statement

John Doe's Net-Worth Statement

Date: January 1, 2014

Assets

Cash in my bank account	$ 2,300
My 401K at work	4,000
Clothes, shoes, personal items	2, 800
Furniture and accessories	3,900
2010 Honda CVR	15,000
Coin Collection	1,000
Total Assets	**$29,000**

Liabilities

Credit Card debt	$ 2,100
Loan from parents	1,900
Car loan	20,000
Total Debt -	**$ 24,000**
Net Worth	**$ 5,000**

Note in this example, the only reason this person has a net worth is because of the value in their clothes, shoes, personal items, furniture and accessories.   This person owes more on their car than it is worth and must pay down the car debt substantially before they could trade the car in or sell it!

I hope that you have a positive number like this example because it is very possible to owe more than what you own. That is called a negative net worth which means you have to pay down some of your debt before you even have a net worth. Many people who rent an apartment or house, who own the contents in their rental home including their personal items, and who are also financing a car that they paid $25,000 for, but today, 2 years after the date they bought the car, is only worth $15,000, could very easily have a negative net worth. When they bought the car, they got a $23,000 loan that they financed for 6 years, and now, two years later the amount of their car loan is still $20,000. They owe $5,000 more than the car is worth. If you add a student loan or credit card debt, their total debt easily exceeds the total value of all the things they own.

Most people have a short period when they are just starting out where they have a negative net worth. Right after graduating from college or a trade school, you haven't even started to earn money yet, however, I want to emphasize "short period". Once you start getting a regular paycheck, you should be focused like a laser beam on building net worth.

The big problem is many people have a negative net worth their entire lives! Most of them will tell you it just happened as though they were a victim of circumstances. Unless you have an awareness of what you are doing with money, you most likely will be in this category. Here are the 2 behaviors that ensure you will never build net worth:

1. You spend every penny that you earn. Also if you get a raise, a tax refund, an inheritance, win the

lottery, etc., you increase your spending until it is all gone. When you do have money left over, you spend freely on vacation trips, eating out, going to movies and shows.

2. The things that you buy have almost no lasting value, or like a car, depreciate quickly after you drive it off the dealer's lot.

If you live with these 2 behaviors, you are basically just a cash flow conduit; money in, and money out until it is all gone. As long as you live this way, you will never have much of a net worth, if any, or any security either.

However, there is a 3rd behavior that many people in the U.S practice daily that will cause this situation to be even worse:

3. Once you have spent everything you earn, you pull out a **credit card** and you go into debt so that you can continue to spend even more. Or, you just spend freely using a credit card and you have no idea how much you have spent until the statement comes in. Not knowing how much you spent causes you to spend way more on credit than you can pay! You also get installment loans to buy the more expensive items, such as cars, furniture, etc.

Let me pose a question: What happens when or if, the cash flow stops? I can tell you. You are broke, bankrupt, and most likely moving into someone's basement. Right now in America, those basements are pretty full.

As I drive through areas of my town, I am amazed at the neighborhoods full of McMansions (large box houses); I see expensive cars everywhere, expensive watches, the latest trendy fashions, top of the market gas grills on stone patios, and much more. Certainly, keeping up with the Jones' is in full gear! Like many of you I often wonder, how do people pay for all of this conspicuous-consumption? Here is the answer: it is all cash flow. Most of these people are spending every penny they make and in a lot of cases, they are deep in debt. Have you ever heard the saying: someone is just a paycheck or two from being completely broke! I think many Americans fall into that category. It is a stressful and troubling way to live, and it rarely ends well.

Having a positive net worth does not mean you are in decent financial condition, however. You may be doing better than the person who has a negative net worth, but you may also still be just as vulnerable to losing a paycheck or two before the bill collectors knock down the door trying to collect money. If you have a positive net worth because you have equity in your home or condo, along with owning some furniture and your personal clothing items, you have nothing to fall back on if something goes wrong. You have to have the major portion of your net worth in savings and investments to have peace of mind about weathering a financial storm.

Yes, you can get a home equity loan, but that is not a real solution to getting through an unexpected financial problem. Borrowing the equity out of your residence just pushes you closer to a negative net worth and you have to have the extra cash flow to pay the debt and interest back.

Having no investments or savings as the major part of your net worth is the real problem.

You notice I said earlier "most of the people" are spending every penny they make. Some people have real wealth. It is not just cash flow. They generally avoid debt, but if they do have some debt, they could pay it all off tomorrow. They mostly pay cash for what they want. Their income exceeds their monthly expenses, and they put that extra money to work in investments. They have 6 months of living expenses in an emergency fund in addition to substantial investments. And yet, they earn comparable incomes to the "spend every penny crowd", sometimes less. They lead purposeful, disciplined lives and make every penny they spend count.

This brings me to Larry's second rule:

2. Debt is the exact opposite of building net worth. Never go into debt unless you have no other choice.

You may feel that is a pretty strong rule but I can tell you that debt is the down fall of millions of Americans today. It is also the reason that approximately 33% of the people in America today over the age of 50 have less than $10,000 saved for retirement.

Loaning money is one of the most lucrative businesses in America. On a street not too far from where I live, I counted 11 banks branches in an approximate one mile section of this busy part of town. In addition to bank branches everywhere, we also have payday lenders, pawn shops, and finance company offices all over our country. No matter where you shop, if you don't have the money to buy something, the store can usually arrange for almost instant credit approval so you can go into debt right on the spot and get what you want.

Getting a loan is so easy most Americans just take it in stride with a dulled awareness of what they are doing to their financial lives and future. Even if you pay your credit card balance off each month, you are still borrowing money. The vendors who accept your credit card pay for the first 30 days of interest for you through fees they pay to the credit card issuer. The credit card companies want you to use that card as often as possible. They know that one day something may happen and you will pay the minimum amount due instead of the full balance, and bingo, they start socking away 12% to 24% interest on the unpaid balance.

Debt is your financial enemy! It is the major reason people do not grow their net worth. That said, not all debt is bad. I feel there are 3 situations where some debt in your life is warranted.

1. Buying a house, condo, townhouse, is just too large a purchase to expect to pay cash. Even saving for a down payment can be daunting. In addition, property holds it value and usually appreciates over time so it is a good purchase. I will have more to say about this in a later chapter.

2. Buying your first car or two. Again, cars are just too expensive to expect to pay cash your first couple of cars. But, unlike your home, a car depreciates

25

rapidly, and will eventually only be worth a small salvage amount.   However, you have to have transportation to get to a job so you can earn a living. Again, I will have more to say about this later in this book.

3. Emergencies. An accident, a health problem that comes out of nowhere, a funeral in a distant place, and other emergencies.

If you start your adult life getting into debt, it is very difficult to ever get out of debt later. In addition to the required expenses of your normal life, everything else has to go to paying down debt for a long period of time in order to become debt free. Plus you have to tear up the credit cards, all of them, and make some major changes to the way you live. And while you are trying to get out of debt, you are vulnerable to any disruption or emergency sinking your debt reduction effort. My advice: never start down the debt road in the first place.

One of the real ironies of life is that if you spend every penny you make, and then also go into debt, you will never have financial security, and never be able to fully retire. You may look rich, like so many people I see today, but in fact, you are actually broke and just a paycheck or two away from financial disaster. I mentioned right before my first rule that you needed to have a plan and goals that are centered in a philosophical understanding of what you want to accomplish in life, and then develop the discipline to reach those goals. Rejecting debt, except for the reasons I earlier listed, is part of that philosophical understanding and discipline. I am going to continue to add to the disciplines that you need and the understanding as we proceed, but controlling and avoiding debt is central to your future success.

I also want to mention that taking on debt is not always as straight forward as you signing a loan or using your credit card. Any time you co-sign on a loan or a credit card with someone else, you just obligated yourself to paying back that debt. Furthermore, if the other person in this debt arrangement defaults, you become the primary debtor by their default. If you cannot pay, then you default and you subject yourself to judgments, liens, and your credit record being marred. Be ready to say no whenever you are asked to co-sign, guarantee, or endorse a loan or debt of any kind.

I also want to point out that I have nothing against having and using credit cards. In our modern way of life they are a great time saver and convenience. But you have to have the discipline to keep track of your spending so that you can pay the entire balance off at the end of each month. In other words, if using credit cards causes you to go into debt, then credit cards are the enemy along with debt. If you find you have a balance left over on your credit card that you cannot pay, put the cards away and use cash or a debit card. If you do use a credit card, please limit yourself to owning one or two cards maximum.

Chapter 3

What Is Financial Security?

There is one more attribute that I earlier mentioned and I want to delve into that now. Your financial goals and planning need to be specific, and by specific, I mean you need to have a dollar amount goal and a time goal. You can grow your net worth without specific goals, but I think you will do a much better job if you have a dollar target and a date to reach that target. This leads me to my next Larry's Rules:

3. Your first long term goal for building Net Worth is to attain financial security. Financial security is the amount of investments you need in order to generate enough income to live without working for a short period of time, (4 to 8 months).

You have probably never asked yourself what is financial security? This rule encompasses the definition of financial security for you. I do not think you have to have enough money invested so that the investment earnings replace your entire current income. If you lost your job suddenly, you would probably cut back on eating out, going to the movies, maybe pare back what level of cable T.V. service you are getting, and just overall tighten up your spending until you got back to work. That reduced level of spending is what I am talking about.

Before I go into how you compute reduced monthly expense, I want to point out to you that I mentioned "your first long term goal" for building net worth. There are actually 4 separate levels of net worth that I want you to consider. Financial security is just the first level and certainly the goal I think everyone must try to attain, and as soon in your adult life as possible. Once you achieve financial security, the next two goals are easier and quicker to accomplish and even more satisfying. See below:

1. Financial Security
2. Financial Independence
3. Retirement
4. Wealthy

I am going to visit all 4 of these net worth levels and I hope I convince you to keep going after you achieve financial security.

To figure out how much you need to save to reach financial security, you have to have a list of everything you spend money on during the month. There are several ways to track spending each month. There are programs you can buy, and apps at the various app stores that you can download to your smart phone or tablet computer, but I have my own way and it is very simple.

First, ask for a receipt for every penny that you spend. Most retailers print a receipt and many times it is just thrown away. Don't let that happen. Ask the cashier to give you a receipt, and any time they ask you if you want a receipt, always say yes. Put those receipts in your purse, your billfold, a secure place, and bring them home. Next record the date, the amount, and what you bought in a small notebook. For many years I kept my notebook with me at all times and recorded my receipts as soon as I spent money, but now I just take the receipts out of my billfold at my desk at home in the evening and record the information in my small notebook. The only issue with not having your notebook with you is every once and a while you are unable to get a receipt. I have been doing this for so long and I am so aware of money being spent, I feel sure I am not missing much, if anything, by not having my notebook with me all the time. Until you get used to writing down all of your purchases, carry your notebook with you. Here is an example of my notebook record:

Exhibit 3.1

Sunday 3/23

Lunch at Panera	$11.00
Ace Hardware, light bulbs	$3.84

Monday 3/24

Gasoline	$28.00

Of course, these are actually hand written entries, but as you can see, I write down the day of the week, the date, and underline it, and then list my purchases for that day. If I did not spend any money that day, I show a big zero. Every day of the month is recorded and underlined. I try to give myself enough information about what I spent the money on so I can categorize it, which leads me to the next step.

In Microsoft Excel, I created a workbook that has 13 worksheets, one for each month of the year and a 13th worksheet where I keep the totals of all the months and some other calculations. In the monthly worksheets I have created categories in the rows so that there is a place to record every penny that I spend each week in the month, and then I also record all of my income at the bottom of the spreadsheet. The categories are open for you to customize to your life. Please take into consideration that too many categories may not tell you anything about broad categories of spending, and on the other hand, not enough categories, may bunch too many things together. You will have to decide how many categories you need, but use my spreadsheets as a guide. I next divide the month up into a maximum of 5 weeks, and then I total everything up at the bottom of that month's page. See the month of May from my Excel workbook in exhibit 3-1, and I also have my 13th worksheet with the yearly totals for you to review in exhibit 3-2.

Every month, just like a business, I close out the month for my records. I have recorded all my spending in categories on my spreadsheet for that month and then total them at the bottom. I subtract my total spending for the month from my income for the month, and then I know to the penny how much I saved or how much over my income I spent. I use the net amount of my paycheck for income because that is all that I control. I get a separate statement for my 401k at work, and the other deductions from my check are already itemized on the pay stub.

If you are married, I recommend that you actually have two spread sheets. See Exhibit 3.3. A separate spreadsheet that covers all joint living expenses such as groceries, utilities, cable T.V., internet access, health insurance, car insurance, mortgage payments, property taxes, child care, etc. Then both husband and wife each have their own personal spreadsheet to track their individual personal expenses such as my personal spreadsheet example in exhibit 3.1. Personal categories would be eating out, all entertainment, prescription drugs, doctor visits, travel, hobbies, clothing, shoes, gasoline, car maintenance, personal drugstore items, magazines, etc. We each make a contribution to pay the joint expenses one time a month based on a budget we worked out, and we have a joint bank account just for those joint expenses. On my personal spreadsheet I show a deduction from my income at the bottom of the sheet that I pay into our joint expense account.

However, if you have a one income family and both of you are comfortable with one spreadsheet then have only one spreadsheet for the two of you, at least for awhile. If you are both working, I think it is advantageous for each person to manage their own personal expenses separately. Men and women have different personal priorities that should not have to be explained to the other party. That said, taking on debt should always be disclosed and discussed. Reaching financial security is a joint goal backed up by a joint plan, even if one party may feel it is a higher priority than the other. Obviously, if you are single, you only need to have one spreadsheet.

The push back I get about tracking expenses is that it takes a lot of time and effort. I don't agree. The most time you are going to spend is in setting up your spreadsheet. That may take an hour or so depending on your proficiency with Excel. No matter if you post your expenses to a spreadsheet weekly or wait and do everything at the end of the month, we are talking about 15 minutes at the most. As for the effort, in my opinion, asking for a receipt every time you spend money is a good thing to do anyway. Awareness of your spending is one of the goals you are trying to accomplish here!

Please keep in mind that all of the numbers in my spreadsheet exhibits are made up. What is important with all the spreadsheet examples is for you to see how the spreadsheets are laid out and how I first total all of the expenses at the bottom, then total all of the income, and then subtract the expenses from the total of the income to see if I have money left over to put in savings. There are Excel spreadsheet formulas in many of the cells but the formulas are all addition or subtractions, so no heavy math is involved.

Exhibit 3.1, Larry's Personal Spreadsheet – see next page.

Larry's Personal Spending

Month: May 2014

Food	Week 1	Week 2	Week 3	Week 4	Totals
Eating Out	$ 105.06	$ 46.05	$ 60.74	$ 35.25	$ 247.10
Eating at Work	$ 12.00	$ 15.00	$ 5.00	$ 5.00	$ 37.00
Total	$ 117.06	$ 61.05	$ 65.74	$ 40.25	$ 284.10

Entertainment	Week 1	Week 2	Week 3	Week 4	Totals
Movie & Popcorn	$ -	$ 18.50	$ -	$ -	$ 18.50
Plays, Musicals, Concerts	$ -	$ -	$ -	$ -	$ -
Tennis	$ 14.00	$ 9.00	$ 9.00	$ 28.00	$ 60.00
Magazines, Books, DVD's	$ 3.75	$ 39.50	$ -	$ -	$ 43.25
Motels & Travel Expense	$ -	$ -	$ -	$ -	$ -
Airline, rental car, train	$ -	$ -	$ -	$ -	$ -
Other Sports	$ -	$ -	$ -	$ -	$ -
Other	$ -				$ -
Total	$ 17.75	$ 67.00	$ 9.00	$ -	$ 121.75

Clothes	Week 1	Week 2	Week 3	Week 4	Totals
Cleaners	$ 28.00	$ -	$ 15.00	$ -	$ 43.00
New clothes	$ -	$ -	$ -	$ -	$ -
New Shoes	$ -	$ 66.00	$ -	$ -	$ 66.00
Total	$ -	$ 66.00	$ -	$ -	$ 109.00

Car Expense	Week 1	Week 2	Week 3	Week 4	Totals
Gasoline	$ 24.51	$ 24.00	$ 25.35	$ 24.30	$ 98.16
Car Wash	$ -	$ 16.50	$ -	$ -	$ 16.50
Maintenance	$ -	$ -	$ -	$ -	$ -
Other	$ -	$ -	$ -	$ -	$ -
Total	$ -	$ 16.50	$ -	$ -	$ 114.66

Exhibit 3.1 Continued

Personal

Church	$ -	$ -	$ -	$ -	$ -
Gifts - Birthday	$ -	$ -	$ 41.00	$ -	$ 41.00
Gifts - Christmas	$ -	$ -	$ -	$ -	$ -
Gifts - Other	$ -	$ -	$ -	$ -	$ -
Postage	$ -	$ -	$ -	$ -	$ -
Drug Store Items	$ -	$ 2.29	$ 43.80	$ -	$ 46.09
Drugs Prescription	$ -	$ -	$ -	$ -	$ -
Doctor's Fees	$ -	$ -	$ -	$ -	$ -
Hobbies - Gardening	$ -	$ 3.84	$ 5.76	$ 23.03	$ 32.63
House Furnishings	$ 59.54	$ -	$ -	$ -	$ 59.54
Cell Phone	$ 25.00	$ -	$ -	$ -	$ 25.00
Other	$ -	$ -	$ -	$ -	$ -
Total	$ 84.54	$ 6.13	$ 90.56	$ 23.03	$ 204.26
Miscellaneous	$ -	$ -	$ -	$ -	$ -
Total Expenses	$ 219.35	$ 216.68	$ 165.30	$ 63.28	$ **833.77**

Wage Income	$ 4,200.00
Monthly Joint Expenses	$ (2,500.00)
Rental Property Net Income	$ 757.21
Other	$ -
Total Income	$ 2,457.21
Subtract Total Spending	$ **833.77**
Net Savings or Loss For The Month	$ **1,623.44**

Exhibit 3.2, Larry's Personal Spreadsheet Totals YTD for 2014 – see next page

Larry's Personal Spending 2014 Totals

	Monthly Net Savings
Jan	$ 1,414.51
Feb	$ 1,704.17
March	$ 1,522.39
April	$ 1,401.00
May	$ 1,623.44
June	$ -
July	$ -
August	$ -
September	$ -
October	$ -
November	$ -
December	$ -
Total Monthly Savings YTD	**$ 7,665.51**

Less

Estmated Tax Payments

Quarterly Tax 2013	$ (1,000.00)
Quarterly Tax 2014	$ (1,400.00)
Total Estimated Taxes	**$ (2,400.00)**

Other One Time Expense and Income

Trip to see sick relative	$ (1,628.00)
Tax Refund for 2013	$ 3,100.00
State Tax Payment 2013	$ (60.00)
Hot water heater replacement	$ (405.00)
New tree planted	$ (300.00)
Bonus For 2013 but paid in 2014	$ 12,356.00
Total One Time Expenses & Income	**$ 13,063.00**

Total Estimated Taxes & One Time Expenses	**$ 10,663.00**
Total Monthly Savings YTD	**$ 7,665.51**
YTD Total Savings	**$ 18,328.51**

Exhibit 3.3, Larry and Mrs. Craig's Combined Spending for May, 2014, and continued on the next page

Larry & Mrs. Craig's Combined Spending
May-14

	Week 1	Week 2	Week 3	Week 4	Total
Food					
Groceries	$ 143.70	$ 141.37	$ 149.22	$ 158.26	$592.55
Utilities & Taxes					
Natural Gas	$ 96.82	$ -	$ -	$ -	$96.82
Electric	$ 69.48	$ -	$ -	$ -	$69.48
Property Taxes	$ 500.00	$ -	$ -	$ -	$500.00
Lawn & Snow Removal	$ -	$ 240.90	$ -	$ -	$240.90
Water & Sewage	$ -	$ 59.47	$ -	$ -	$59.47
Total	$666.30	$300.37	$0.00	$0.00	$966.67
Communications					
Telephone	$0.00	$ -	$ -	$ -	$0.00
Newspaper	$ -	$ -	$ -	$ -	
Internet	$24.95	$ -	$ -	$ -	$24.95
Cable TV	$83.93	$ -	$ -	$ -	$83.93
Total	$108.88	$0.00	$0.00	$0.00	$108.88
Medical Insurance					
Health Insurance	$0.00	$0.00	$ -	$ -	$0.00
Dental Insurance	$ -	$ -	$ -	$ -	$0.00
Total	$0.00	$0.00	$0.00	$0.00	$0.00
Property Insurance					
For 2 Cars	$125.00	$ -	$ -	$ -	$125.00
Homeowners	$100.00	$ -	$ -	$ -	$100.00
Other	$ -	$ -	$ -	$ -	$0.00
Total	$225.00	$0.00	$0.00	$0.00	$225.00

Exhibit 3.3 Continued

Household & Other

House Cleaning	$85.00	$ -	$ -	$ -	$85.00
Mortgage Payment	$1,225.00	$ -	$ -	$ -	$1,225.00
Community Asso. Dues	$75.00	$ -	$ -	$ -	$75.00
Light bulbs, batteries, etc.	$0.00	$ -	$ 24.16	$ -	$24.16
Home Improvement	$100.00	$ -	$ -	$ -	$100.00
Insecticide, Roundup, etc.	$ 9.55	$ -	$ -	$ -	$9.55
Total	$1,494.55	$0.00	$24.16	$0.00	$1,518.71
Weekly Totals	$2,638.43	$441.74	$173.38	$158.26	**$3,411.81**

Our Joint Monthly Contributions	$3,500.00
Other	$0.92
Other	
Total Income	$3,500.92
Subtract Total Spending	**$3,411.81**
Amount Left Over	**$89.11**

NOTE

Notice the amounts under property tax, car insurance, homeowners insurance, and home improvements. They show up in a separate reserves box on the year-end spreadsheet, as shown in Exhibit 3.4, on the next page.

Exhibit 3.4, Larry and Mrs. Craig's Year End Totals for Their Combined Monthly Spreadsheets

Combined Totals	
	Totals
January	$98.22
February	$102.00
March	($106.79)
April	$55.41
May	$89.11
June	$0.00
July	$0.00
August	$0.00
September	$0.00
October	$0.00
November	$0.00
December	$0.00
Total	$ 237.95

Exhibit 3.4 Continued with Larry and Mrs. Craig's Reserve spreadsheet

Reserves and Actual Expenses

	2013	2014	2014	2014 YTD
	Surplus From Last Year	Add To Reserve	Actual Expenses	Surplus
Property Tax	$ 4,065.79	$ 2,500.00	$ -	$ 6,565.79
Car Insurance	$ 1,893.26	$ 625.00	$ (516.49)	$ 2,001.77
Homeowners Insurance	$ 266.62	$ 500.00	$ -	$ 766.62
Home Improvement	$ 1,386.41	$ 500.00	$ (324.95)	$ 1,561.46
Overage	$ 108.33	$ 237.95	$ -	$ 346.28
Totals	$ 7,720.41	$ 4,362.95	$ (841.44)	$ 11,241.92

Actual Home Improvement Expenses

Garage Door Repair	$ (175.00)
Sprinkler System Repair	$ (149.95)
Total Home Improvement	**$ (324.95)**

I want to address a couple of questions you may have about when and where to post some of your spending. If you spend with a credit card, you should post the spending at the time of purchase, not when you get your monthly credit card bill. If you buy tickets for a show that is two months out, you post the spending the day you spend the money, not when you actually go to see the musical, or play. As a general rule, whenever you actually spend money, it goes in your notebook and later, on to your spreadsheet.

If you do not have Microsoft Excel, you can also keep the spreadsheet manually. Just buy column paper at an office supply store, and get a calculator to add and subtract. It will take you a bit longer to fill it in, but it will accomplish the same thing.

I accrue a reserve for large expenses. For instance, my homeowners insurance is paid once a year, however, I put down $100 a month as expense, and then I keep a little side spreadsheet of all my reserves. I subtract the actual cost of the insurance when I pay it on my side spreadsheet from the reserve amount.   I actually accrue reserves for several things such as, $100 a month for home improvements, $125 for automobile insurance, and $500 for property tax. By having the money set aside for these large expenses, I am not caught off guard when the bill comes in.   Also, I am spreading this expense out over the year so that it does not all fall in one month. In some cases, like property tax that goes up and down each year, I have reserved more than I need, so I have some extra money accumulated to use somewhere else when needed.   I used to reserve for vacations, and some other items, but once I attained financial independence, it was no longer necessary.

This brings me to another Larry's Rules:

4. Track your spending and income every month, and total it for the year, hopefully forever, but for sure until you reach your long term goals. You need to know whether you reached your savings goal for that month, and more importantly for the year.

I want you to track your income and expenses forever! Let me tell you just some of the benefits. If you are not reaching your savings goal, you can go right to your trusty spreadsheet and review your spending to find out where your money went. Maybe it was a onetime expense, or maybe you are spending more at the grocery store each month, or buying more gasoline, or eating out at more expensive restaurants. You can use your spreadsheet to spot areas of spending where you know you can cut back, like your cable T.V, your cell phone expense, or buying too many bakery goods that aren't even good for you. Many people know they are spending too much money each month but without a monthly spreadsheet, they have no real idea where the problem is. I guarantee you will be surprised at how much you are actually spending in more than one category. I certainly was.

Finally, let's discuss your savings goal. After a few months of using your spread sheet, you now know what it cost you to live each month. As I mentioned earlier, see if there are a few areas you could cut back if you lost your job. For example, let's say you are single and your average monthly spending is $3,100. You figure if you lost your job you could get by each month with $2,700. The $400

44

reduction in expenses would be saved from less eating out, less gasoline, reduced cable T.V., and some other non-essential spending.

So you need enough in investments that would earn you $2,700 a month, or $32,400 a year. Next you have to make an assumption about the return or interest rate you can get on your savings/investments. Returns are low at the moment so I am going with 6%. All you need to do to calculate your financial security savings amount is divide $32,400 by .06, and you get $540,000. It is a big number but this is what you need to save. Let's test our math:

$540,000

X .06   (6%)

$32,400 perfect!

The return that you get on your investments makes a big difference in the target amount you need to save. Let's say you can average a 9% return instead of 6%. Your savings goal would be lowered to $360,000. Studies going back nearly 100 years show the long term return for a portfolio 100% invested in the stock market are approximately 11% a year. As we know, history does not always repeat itself, especially right now, and being 100% invested in stocks is way too risky, so a conservative 6% is our target return, especially now when interest rates are almost at zero.

You are not going to save $540,000 quickly. It is going to take awhile. Remember this is a long term goal. I am using a Hewlett Packard 12C finance calculator to do all of my calculations in this book but you can use any calculator that will compute future and present values. Here is a listing of how long it will take you to reach financial security, depending on the amount you can save per month:

Number of years to save \$540,000

- \$400 per month, at 6%   = 34 years
- \$600 per month at 6%   = 29 years
- \$800 per month at 6%   = 25 years
- \$1,000 per month at 6%   = 22 years
- \$1,500 per month at 6%   = 17 years
- \$2,000 per month at 6%   = 15 years

There are two variables in figuring how long it will take you to reach your goal: 1. the amount that you can save each month, 2. the rate of return. You really only have control of one of those variables and that is the amount you can save per month.

Your financial security amount that you are saving for will increase over time, not only because of inflation, but also because over the years your cost of living will increase. On the good side, your investment returns may have gone up as well. In any case, every 5 years you need to revisit your goal and make adjustments based on your actual living cost at the time and hopefully you will also be making more and therefore, saving more.

I am not the first person to recommend tracking your expenses and income. Many people in the 19th and 20th centuries kept track of their spending. John D. Rockefeller Senior kept what he called a ledger on him at all times where he recorded every penny he spent, and he attributed his great wealth to knowing exactly where he was financially by just opening up his ledger. I first learned how to do this from a magazine article and at first I tried it just for a couple of months as the article suggested. A few months later I decided to run my personal financial life just like you would any business. I needed to know monthly how much progress I was making towards my long term net worth goals. I asked myself if I would work for any company where all they kept was a checkbook register with a list of checks and the balance totaled. Any business with this minuscule of information does not even know if it made a profit each month and has all of the problems any individual does in not knowing where money is disappearing each month. So I decided to continue with my spreadsheet every month and to have at least the basic knowledge of how much I spent, how much I saved, and how much progress I was making in reaching my financial goals. The pay-off for me versus the small amount of time it took me each month has really been unbelievable. It has been like stepping out of the dark and into the light. I was able to see my savings grow and to vigorously reduce my spending. I was also able to project more accurately when I would achieve my goal of financial security. I still track my spending every month and it is just as helpful now even though I am financially independent.

I cannot describe to you how good it feels to see your net worth climb every month, and every year. When I saved my first $100,000, it was a break through moment for me and I knew I was finally on the right track with my financial goals. Five years into my plan, I slept better at night, I felt more confident at work, and I finally felt that the daily grind of my job was about more than what happened that day or that week. All of those feelings made the saving just that much easier and my enthusiasm for the whole process increased. After 5 years, it became a way of life for me, and I reached my goal several years before I had originally planned. One other thing, as your investable funds grow, the growth in your balance begins to take on momentum. There comes a point when the monthly amount you earn on your investments exceeds the monthly amount you are putting into savings each month. Your balance really takes off like a rocket at that point.

Chapter 4

Where Do I Save?

I am a proponent of having much of your savings done on auto pilot. That means having it deducted from your paycheck before you ever have a chance to spend it. Here is my next Larry's Rules:

5. **If you have a 401K or 403B retirement savings plan available at work, put 10% of your salary into it on day one or increase your contribution to 10% as soon as possible. No more, no less. If there is no retirement plan at work, then open an Individual Retirement Account (IRA) for yourself and put 10% away.**

If you follow my rule, you automatically save 10% of what you earn before you even get your paycheck. The beauty of these retirement plans is that they reduce your taxable income, so you actually reduce your income tax by participating. If you are not at 10% where you work now or in your own IRA, get there as soon as you can.

With a lot of 401K plans, your employer offers incentives for participating. Where I worked, the first 4% of my salary I put into the plan was matched fifty cents on the dollar by my company. So right off the bat I got a 50%

return on part of my 10% contribution! Even if there is no incentive, put 10% in as a rule.

Why did I add "no more or no less" than 10%? Because I want you to have substantial savings outside of your retirement plans at work and also after taxes have been paid. You need to have an emergency fund, savings for a house down payment, car down payment, and most importantly, I want you to have a large after tax savings/investment balance as part of your financial security plan. If you ever have to actually use your savings to live on for a while, I do not want you to ever go into your 401K or 403B, or Individual Retirement Account (IRA) early. In that regard here is another rule:

6. Never take money out of your retirement plans before you are age 59 and ½.

I am not going to spend a lot of time on this rule because I think it is self-explanatory. Taking money out early not only undermines your long term goals but you have to pay a 10% income tax penalty in addition to paying regular income tax on the withdrawal. If you follow this plan, you will have monies saved outside of retirement plans that you can use in an emergency. And of course, this prohibition would also apply to borrowing against your 401K.

Maybe not the first day you start a job but certainly after you have bought a car, furnished your apartment, and you are settled in a place, I want you to set a goal of saving a minimum of 20% of your income per year. And that is one of Larry's Rules:

7. Your minimum savings goal including retirement savings is 20% of your gross salary each year.

I know 20% sounds like a lot and again, I am not suggesting that you save that amount on day one of your first job, but as soon as possible after you adopt my rules, that is where I want you to be. Here is how you get there without too much pain.

When you get a raise, put half of the amount you receive in your paycheck into savings. If you get a bonus, put 100% into savings. A bonus is a onetime windfall and your monthly income already covers your expenses, so it is money you can afford to save. If you change jobs and substantially increase your salary, put half into savings until you reach your 20% goal. If you get a tax refund, right into savings. Remember, you are not going to save money for the rest of your life. Once you achieve your goals, you can reassess what you want to do, but until you at least have financial security, what could be more important?

I realize that the amount that you earn is an important factor in how much you save and also the sacrifice you will have to make to your standard of living. A single person making $50,000 a year is going to have to make some real sacrifices to save 20% a year. For a single person making $100,000 per year, the change in their standard of living is almost negligible. Even after saving $20,000 a year, or more than twice what the person making $50,000 per year will save, you will still have $80,000 left to pay all expenses.

Another factor is children. We all know children are very expensive to feed, clothe, educate, etc. However, the best gift you could ever give to your children is that they never have to help you financially, or worry about you, or have you live with them later because you cannot take care of yourself. It will be tough saving 20% with children at home, but with a little sacrifice and stretching a dollar until it screams it can be done. At the same time you are modeling behavior that hopefully your children will adopt in their adult lives.

I am asking you to save 20% minimum per year, but there is nothing holding you back from saving more. I saved over 30% of my income all through my 40's. Many people in other parts of the world regularly save 30% or more each year. I am sad to say America is one of the few countries in the world that has experienced a negative savings rate as a nation! Certainly, if you make a large income you will want to exceed 20% per year. Remember achieving financial security is your first long term savings goal. Once you reach that goal, you next need to continue saving to reach your other goals, which I will cover shortly.

Many people meet their financial security goal in less than 15 years. If you follow my suggestions for saving bonuses, tax refunds, and half of your raises, it can be done. Some married couples who both work, live on one salary, and save 100% of the other salary. If you both agree, this is a great way to accelerate your savings. One other variable to consider that I will detail later in this book, is how much it cost you to live each month. You have to try to keep a reasonable lid on that spending number until you reach your goal.

This brings me to another Larry's Rules.

8. Periodically, review the list of benefits that come from achieving financial security.

I understand that saving 20% of your income (or more) takes a lot of discipline and sacrifice, but there is also a lot to celebrate and just plain feel good about. I want to list some of the benefits for you to review when you feel it is getting tough.

1. Worry over money subsides, therefore you sleep better.
2. If you get let go at work, you have a nest egg to rely on until you find another job.
3. You are more confident about speaking up for yourself or asking for a raise at work because you have financial security.
4. If a once in a lifetime business opportunity comes along, you can consider taking part because you have some funds to invest.
5. You need additional training for a better job and now you can afford to take classes at night.
6. Something you want to buy offers a large discount if you pay cash. No problem, you have savings.
7. You are completely burnt out at work and need a sabbatical but your company does not offer one. You have the ability to recharge your batteries for a while, or as mentioned earlier, you have the resources to train for another higher paying, less stressful job.

8. You would like to retire early. You already have a head start on your plan. All you need to do is calculate the extra amount you need and then continue to save as much as you can.
9. Your credit score is excellent because you have the resources to pay all of your bills on time. And you have no or very little debt.
10. You get a call from someone very close to you saying they are near death and you want to visit before they are gone. You have the resources to make that trip.
11. You see home-less people on a visit to the city. You never have to worry about that for yourself.
12. Your car dies on you. No problem, you have savings so you can get it fixed immediately or you trade it in. This also applies to your hot water heater, refrigerator, air-conditioner, washing machine, dryer, etc.

To sum it up, if you look at the list above and add it all up, the major benefit of having financial security is freedom. The freedom to be who you really want to be, the freedom to say what you really want to say, the freedom to make changes in your life, and the freedom that comes from being secure with everything that you need to survive and prosper. I could go on but I think by now you should be seeing the clear benefits of staying the course with your savings.

Chapter 5

Financial Independence, Retirement, and Wealthy

In my 30's, when I finally figured out what long term goals to set for myself, I knew right off that financial security was not enough for me. I wanted to have options to do whatever I wanted to do if something happened to my job. I will tell you more about my story as I cover financial independence.

Financial Independence

The difference between financial security and independence is that your goal is to live without a job indefinitely and not make any adjustments to the way you live. In my example earlier in this book, I showed you a single person who had total expenses of $3,100, and in an emergency we figured that person could easily reduce their spending by $400 a month. If financial independence is your goal, we are going to add the $400 back into expenses and plan for investment income to cover all of your expenses. Also part of your financial independence goal is to pay off all of your debts, including your mortgage before you live independently. So, I am going to reduce expenses by $1,000 per month because in my earlier example of a single person, their monthly expenses included a condo mortgage that will now be paid off and also a car payment of $250 per month which will be paid off. So the new monthly expense is $1,850 per month. See on the next page.

Total Monthly Expense With Out Condo Mortgage or Car Payment

Beginning Monthly Expense	$3,100
Less Car Payment	- 250
Less Condo Mortgage Payment	- 1,000
New Monthly Expense	**$1,850**

When you live independently, until you reach age 59 and a half, all of your income will come out of your after tax savings and investments. Your 401K, 403B, or IRA will just keep building. You will only incur income taxes on the amount you earn on your after tax savings and investments. If you are primarily in mutual funds and exchange traded funds, which I recommend, your realized income from your investments is going to be low. Remember with stock type investments you are only taxed when you sell or when the mutual fund you own realizes a capital gain, or when dividends are paid. So, I am only going to put down $200 per month for state and federal tax, but you will have to see as you go along what income you actually get. You will no longer be saving money so there is no adjustment for savings. Also no social security tax deduction will be made because you are living off of investments and you only pay social security tax on payroll income. One addition is for health insurance. Your employer most likely subsidizes your insurance so health insurance expense will be much higher. As I earlier mentioned, you need to shop for the best health insurance value you can find. This time I am adding $800 per month for health insurance. See my calculations below:

Adjusted Monthly Expenses to Live Independently

Total monthly expenses	$1,850
Health Insurance (estimate)	+ 800
State & Federal tax estimate (12%)	+ 200

New Independent Monthly Expense   **$2,850**

We are still not finished. Remember the accruals I made each month in my spreadsheet so that I spread out a large expense by building a reserve, we need to do that here. I want to add several additional accruals. One for dental expense of $20 per month or $240 per year, eye exams and glasses at $20 per month, car repair and new tires $30 per month, vacations $100 per month, and a reserve for the interior of the condo this person owns of $80 per month. Eventually you have to replace carpets, dish washer, refrigerator, stove, air-conditioner, etc. See on the next page.

Adjusted Monthly Expense with Added Reserve Accruals

Beginning Adjusted Monthly Expense	$2,850

Add

Dental	20
Eye exams & glasses	20
Car repair, new tires, oil changes	30
Vacation	100
Condo interior replacements	80

New Monthly Expense with Reserves $3,100

Now we can figure the amount you need to save so that investment earnings will cover your monthly expenses. I am going to the $3,100 and multiply by 12 so we have an annual amount needed. That amount is $37,200. Just divide $37,200 by .06, our investment return of 6%, and you get a savings amount of $620,000. Again a large number but not that much more than the $540,000 we needed to achieve financial security.

I have one last addition to your financial independence savings goal. You have to take into consideration that you do not intend to work or save any more, so I think you need to also add a reserve amount to cover inflation, medical expenses, or any other unexpected expense. I would add at a minimum another $100,000 to your goal to make sure you are covered. So your total savings goal is $720,000.

As I previously mentioned, I have assumed that all major debts are paid off. If you are going to live independently you need to pay off your mortgage and also pay off your car loan or you are going to have to save a much higher amount. It is amazing how much cheaper you are able to live with those major debts paid off. That is why I highly recommend that you concentrate on paying off your mortgage at the earliest date possible. Later, in the spending section of this book, I will give you my ideas on how to do that.

I am not recommending that you retire early. Your goal is to have the **option** to retire before normal retirement age. I define normal retirement age as 67 because that is when you can receive full social security benefits. Earlier in my life I really thought retiring as soon as you could was a good and worthy goal. I no longer feel that way. Here are my reasons. At age 45, or 50, or 55 even, you have just too much experience and plain know-how to let it go to waste by retiring at one of those ages. Use your gifts and talents to make more money (you can never have too much) and to contribute to society. If you have worked at the same company for a long time, you most likely will have a good amount of vacation time, and if you have saved for independence, you no longer need to be stressed out about keeping your job. Keep on working and being engaged. If you are in good health, you most likely will live to age 90 or longer so you will have plenty of time to do what you want after you retire.

Another reason not to retire too early is boredom and loneliness. Say you are able to retire at age 50. You can find a lot of people to do things with during the day, but most likely your new friends are going to be age 68, 72, 79, etc. Your contemporaries, the people you have the most in common with, are back at the office still working trying to meet their goals. Moreover, if you retire even later, say at age 60, and live to age 90, you still will have a 30 year retirement. That is a lot of years taking it easy!

My last reason is that being challenged and contributing to your company's mission keeps you sharp and alive. I think working a bit longer actually lengthens your life and certainly enriches it.

Another option to consider is to use your financial independence to do something you have always wanted to do. I know several people who have decided to leave their career job and teach school for several years before they retire. Others have pursued other passions they have always wanted to do, such as running for a political office, or working in an entirely different field. By achieving financial independence you have given yourself a multitude of options.

At age 65 or any age after 65, go for it, fully retire. You are now old enough to fit in with the retired crowd even though they will treat you as a youngster. At this age, you will start on Medicare which should reduce your insurance cost. You are also much closer to starting your social security checks coming in and when you do start, it will take some of the burden off your savings and investments.

Of course, the numbers in the examples in this book are all made up. My purpose was to demonstrate to you the process, the items that need to be included, and to get you familiar with the amount of money you are going to have to save. Everyone has a different set of expenses that have to be considered and factored into their financial independence calculation. If you are married, you also have to see if both parties are on board with the plan and then make accommodations for both parties. Many times one party wants to continue working longer than the other person, or one spouse is just not on board at all.

I did all of these same calculations for myself in my late 30's. I cannot express to you the change this made in the course of my life. It changed everything for me. While I was saving during those years, I called the figure I was saving for my FREEDOM DAY amount. As the dollars really began to build up near the end of my goal, I felt that load that so many people feel on their shoulders begin to lift. I was no longer subject to the ups and downs of my employer. And it was a good thing. Six months after I left my career job, my company was merged with another company and nearly everyone in my office was terminated! There was a severance package but it was significantly reduced. Luckily, I did not have to go through the stress of being let go. Most of the people I worked with had been transferred to my office, so not only did they not have a job any longer but they had to sell their home and pay to get themselves back to where they were from. Unfortunately, this is not an unusual occurrence in America today.

Now, I did not leave my job intending to never work again. My plan was to work part-time and I did until I fully retired at age 62. When I say part time, I worked 32 hours or more a week, so it was just barely part time, however my employers went along with me having a 3 day weekend every week, but they did not like it. I think it would be harder today to find good paying part time work, maybe impossible.

Because we had no debt, even with just part time work for me, and my wife continued to work full time, I was still able to save 15% of my income most of those years. Not having any debt just makes everything come together.

Retirement

Your planning for financial independence is essentially retirement planning. The only difference is accounting for social security income, possibly pension income, and health care. Actually health care in retirement is still one of the more complicated areas. You get Medicare at age 65 but you will need a Medicare Supplement. For planning purposes I would calculate supplement expense using Plan F, which is the most comprehensive supplement plan. All of the supplement plans are identical no matter which insurance company you choose or where you live in the U.S. However, each company is free to charge whatever they want for the policy so shopping around is imperative. You will also need to figure in Medicare drug plan coverage. You can get estimates for these policies by calling any of the major health insurance companies such as Blue Cross, Blue Shield, United Healthcare, or go to Medicare.gov where you can compare all of the supplement cost.

If you retire early (pre age 65), you will have to investigate health insurance through the Affordable

Healthcare Act (Obamacare). There are a lot of on-line resources to help you choose a policy and then find out how much it will cost. You need to have a monthly expense amount and also figure in any deductible that you are required to pay first so that you can accurately plan your early exit from the work force.

For retirement, you have to have additional funds to cover the cost of replacing cars, house repairs, travel, and to cover out of pocket medical expense. A minimum of $100,000 and possibly more would be optimal. If you have saved for a goal of financial independence, you are all set for retirement once you start drawing social security or a pension. I just want to emphasize that the amount of your expenses is going to go up over time, so the amount you need to save is going to go up as well. If you start your savings plan at age 30, then you need to every 5 years make adjustments to your plans that take into consideration that your expenses are going to be higher when you actually retire in 25 or 30 years.

Wealthy

If being wealthy is your goal, it all comes down to your ability to earn a large income and at the same time keep your cost of living low. Someone making $15,000 per month with $3,100 total monthly expenses like my single person example, could after taxes save approximately $7,000 per month. Just 10 years of savings with a 6% return would build $1.1 million. If you increase the investment return to 8%, you would have just shy of $1.3 million. Or save for 15 years and you will have $2,036,000 with a 6% return or twice as much saved than after 10 years. The exponential nature of compounding takes over once you have a large amount of savings and investment, and then wealth builds dramatically.

If you make a large income, there is one professional person that you will need to see more often and that is a tax adviser. Just remember, do not let saving taxes get you off your goal of building net worth. For instance, a tax adviser may point out that you could buy a larger house with a larger mortgage, and that would give you a larger mortgage interest deduction. If your primary reason for buying a larger house is just to get a larger tax deduction, then don't do it. Here is better plan. Pay off your condo mortgage and then rent out the property, buy another condo, and then do it all over again. There are many more tax considerations and options if you are in a high income tax bracket just make sure your tax saving choices support you goals.

What size net worth do you need to say you are wealthy? I do not have a set amount to give you. I would say that if you have a net worth that is 4 or 5 times more than you need to live the same life style you are living now, you are doing quite well. Being wealthy is not everyone's goal, and in my mind, just saving to achieve financial security by age 50 or 55, is enough for most people and a tough challenge.

Chapter 6

How Do I Get A 6% Return?

I mentioned earlier that I have made a lot of mistakes in growing my net worth over the years, and investing is the one area where I have made the most mistakes. I was fortunate though, because during most of my investing years interest rates were sky high so that even sitting in a money market fund paid a lot more that investing in a 30 year corporate bond today.

Investing can be one of the most confusing, and exasperating things you can get involved with, but it doesn't have to be. I have tried just about everything and I have read a ton of books on it, and I have come to some hard earned lessons and conclusions about what is the right thing to do, and the wrong thing to do.

First of all, I want to tell you that during your working years, you only have a limited amount of time left over after working all day for what I consider to be some truly important activities, such as: family time, some physical fitness time, and some leisure time with friends, or hobbies. Your time is best spent doing what benefits your life the most, and I can tell you reading, studying, and speculating on the stock market is **not** one of those things that is going to better your life. You can spend a lot of wasted time on it and not improve your investing results, and worse, lose a lot of money in the process. I have tried a bunch of things and lost money doing most of them. In my case, I stopped doing them quickly before the losses mounted. Not everyone is so fortunate.

No one knows what course the future is going to take. We can guess, and we can act like we confidently know the future, but like a lot of the talking heads on financial television shows, their pontificating on what to invest in right now to take advantage of the next trend actually has a very low success rate. You and I know those investment gurus really have an agenda, and that is to get their hands on your money. Just remember no one has a crystal ball.

Here is a list of the things I tried that either lost money or at best, were a complete waste of time:

- Buying individual stocks.
- Timing the markets, both selling and buying.
- Buying stocks on margin (borrowing money from your broker to buy more stock).
- Churning, or buying and selling in less than 6 months.
- Day trading.
- Investment newsletters.
- Selling stocks short.
- Buying and selling options (puts and calls) on stocks.
- Buying Exchange Traded Funds (ETF's) that invest in commodities, precious metals, currencies, and other odd categories.

- Buying Exchange Traded funds that have 2 to 1 or even 3 to 1 leverage both on the upside of stocks and the downside for stocks.
- Buying based on talking heads advice on the financial shows on T.V.
- Buying based on tips from anyone!

I think you can get the idea from my list of what does not work. Some of the things I listed above do work for some investors, but I can tell you they are most likely full time investors and traders who are obsessed with investing. And even they get wiped out sometimes by doing what is on my list.

Here is what does work and it is so simple that it is hard to accept. Invest in 5 or 6 broad categories of stocks through mutual funds or exchange traded funds, and then never sell! Just think about it, buying stock is actually buying a piece of a for-profit corporation. A corporation that is plotting, planning, researching, experimenting with everything it can to make money. Just like you are doing in the business you work in. All you need to do is spread your risk by buying into a wide category of stocks and then let these corporations do their thing over a long period of time. In trying to make more income for themselves, these companies are building wealth for you.

This is one of Larry's Rules:

9. Invest in Exchange Traded Funds or Mutual Funds that cover 5 or 6 broad categories of stocks and bonds by dollar cost averaging in and then never sell.

Let's break this rule down. What is dollar cost averaging? It is simply investing a fixed amount of money every month, or every quarter so that as the market falls and rises, you buy in at different prices over time. This method insures that you do not put all of your money in at the top of the market. Instead, you end up with an average price for your investments. Investing in a company 401K, 403B, or your own IRA each month is dollar cost averaging and it is a good thing to do.

Here are the 5 broad categories that I want you to be invested in:

1. Large capitalized U.S. companies. Basically the Standard and Poor's 500.
2. Small or mid capitalized U.S. companies.
3. International large companies
4. Emerging Market companies.
5. Real Estate through Real Estate Investment Trust

This mix ensures that you are invested in top companies all over the world and it simplifies your investing. It also ensures that you are invested in just about every major industry. And best of all it works. Long term studies show that people who invest in this manner grab nearly all of the true returns the market produces in its major indexes, and you will also enjoy low investing cost. All of that puts more money in your pocket. But the best benefit of this strategy is that you can go about your daily life and do the things that earn you more money, and bring more joy to your life.

First of all, let me say that I do not favor ETF's over mutual funds, or vice-versa. ETF's primarily invest in market indexes like the Dow Jones Industrials or the Standard & Poor's 500. The major benefit of this type of investing is very low cost, indexes beat 80% of all mutual funds and financial advisers, broad diversification, and minimal buying and selling. However, the companies that manage the indexes do make changes based on rules they have set for the index. The cons of ETF's are that you have no chance of beating the market, and there is no investment manager watching day to day events.

For mutual funds the pros are wide diversification, moderate cost, professionally managed, and may beat the market indexes. The cons are they cost more than ETF's, also, the cost may be hidden, there are too many choices of funds, and sometimes too much buying and selling in the fund. So, it comes down to basically low cost versus having a manager that cost more. Both work great over long periods of time, and there is no reason you cannot have some of both. With that covered, let's move on.

Here is how you implement this strategy. And let me first say, you are going to have a slightly different investment strategy for your 401K, 403B, or IRA, than the funds you save from your paycheck and after taxes have been paid. First let's invest the money you save at work. I want you to just start at the top of the list shown above and put 100% of your money into large cap U.S. companies. When you have $10,000 invested in that category, then go to the next category and save $10,000, and then the next category with $10,000. Once you have $10,000 in each category, just start all over again and add another $10,000 to each category. I want you to repeat this process over and over again until you hit age 40. You are going to be 100% in stocks until age 40.

At age 40, I want you to add fixed income investments into the mix. Put 100% of your money into a short term bond fund until you have 20% of your total investments in that fund. Say, at age 40 for instance, you have $200,000 in stock investments, so put your next $40,000 in savings into a short term bond fund by dollar cost averaging in. At age 50, I want you to increase fixed income to 30% of the total value of your retirement fund balance. After age 60, your goal is 50% fixed income and 50% in stocks, and you will stay with that percentage all through your retirement years.

The only thing else you need to do is rebalance your retirement portfolio if one category out grows the others by 10% or more but I only want you to do that once every year. Here is a look at an evenly balanced portfolio at age 40, with your $200,000 total invested as shown below.

Large cap US stocks	$40,000
Small or mid cap US stocks	40,000
International Stocks	40,000
Emerging Markets	40,000
Real Estate REITS	40,000
Total Investments	**$200,000**

One of the drawbacks of 401K and 403B accounts is that they usually have limited investment choices. Almost all of these plans will have choices that cover most of my categories but maybe not all. In that case you are going to have to work with what they give you. Every retirement plan has a large cap or an S & P 500 mutual fund or ETF. Most of them will have a mid cap or small cap investment choice. If they have both available, I prefer small cap over mid cap, but whatever one you decide on, just one fund for this category. Most plans will have either a Global Fund or International Fund. Always go with the fund that has International in the name. Global funds sometimes allow 50% of the stocks to be U.S. stocks and you already have that covered. What may be harder to find is an Emerging Market Fund. You can substitute an International small cap fund for that fund if they have one. If not, you are just out of luck in that category. A real estate mutual fund may also be hard to find as an investment choice. If they do not have real estate, you can substitute a dividend income fund.

If your company does not have a retirement plan, you should have your own Individual Retirement Account (IRA). Any large mutual fund/brokerage company can help you set one up. I have a list of my favorite 4 companies in the next paragraph.

If your company offers a target date fund in your savings plan, you may want to choose it and scrap the plan I outlined above. A target date fund is a mutual fund that targets the year that you plan to retire. Say 2040, and they diversify and allocate your savings for you. I like this choice especially if your savings plan is with one of my 4 top investment companies listed later in this chapter.

Let's now get into what you want to do with the 10% of your income you are saving on your own. Your first priority is to have an emergency fund. My suggestion is to have at a minimum, 6 months of living expenses that you can tap at any time. In my earlier example, my single person needed $2,700 per month just to get by while out of a job. So, 6 months means that person would need to have $16,200 somewhere safe and accessible (let's round up to $17,000). Personally I would do a bit more, like 10 or 12 months of expenses, just in case you have a hard time finding a new job. Your next task is to open a brokerage account. Here are the 4 large, well known companies I recommend:

1. Charles Schwab
2. Fidelity Investments
3. T. Rowe Price Investments
4. Vanguard Investments

I put them in alphabetical order. I do not really favor one over the other, they are all excellent. After you make your choice, give them a call and open an investment account. Have them put the first deposit into your account into a money market account. You want to always have some of your emergency funds in a money market account. The rest of your emergency fund can go into a short term corporate bond fund.

All of the companies I listed above have checking accounts available so you can write a check against your emergency funds. All you need to do is transfer $2,000 into your newly opened bank account that is located with your brokerage account, in case you need it in an emergency.

Usually the first order of blank checks is free. And the brokerage company will help you do this.

Once you have saved your emergency fund in a combination of bank account, money market account and short term corporate bond fund, you are set to start investing in stocks. You can follow the same process I laid out for your at work savings plan, or I have another suggestion.

There is an alternative for your after tax savings, and it is low cost and it is much easier to implement rather than doing it yourself. It is called robo advisors. Based on your age, and the amount you have saved, they have a mathematical asset allocation worked out for you that diversifies your money broadly using primarily Exchange Traded Funds. There are two companies that are the leaders in this business: Wealthfront and Betterment. Their fees are very low at around .25% of the amount invested and they do everything else for you. They allocate across all of the categories that I have in my plan, and they also handle fix income investments. They automatically re-balance for you, and they automatically change the asset allocation as you age to a higher amount of fix income. I have previewed their asset allocation and their investment choices, and I feel they do an excellent job. You can find both of these companies on the internet. The brokerage companies are also starting to get into Robo investing but the two companies I mentioned pioneered this concept and have the lowest expenses.

If you decide to invest your after-tax savings or even you own IRA by yourself, I will give you a sample portfolio using ETF's, and then the same portfolio using mutual funds in the index in the back of this book. Use my suggestions as a guide. There are other mutual funds and ETFs that also do a good job. If you need help in choosing a mutual fund, you can use Morningstar at your local library as an expert guide.

That is all you need to know about investments to grow your net worth right in-line with the major market index returns. You probably noticed I did not mentioned whether the economy is in a recession or not, or the market is setting records or not. It just does not really matter for this plan to work over a long period of time. Since we have the whole world covered with investments, hopefully something is growing all of the time, and if it isn't, then it will be in the near future. Best of all, you will be investing each month while waiting for stocks to take off again. You do need to know that stocks can fluctuate wildly, and you may have losses for an extended period of time. Just keep dollar cost averaging in so that you are buying as much as you can while stocks are cheap. My advice is to not look at your stock balance too often. Just let your investments build and do not stray from this plan.

If you find you cannot sleep at night with this plan, then you need to go another route which is totally safe investments, like bank CD's and savings accounts. However, you are going to suffer lower long term returns if you go for total safety. Most likely, less than half the returns you would get from stocks in the long run. You have to know yourself and do what is right for you.

Every 4 or 5 years, we have a bear market where all stocks go down for a period of time. A bear market is where the major indexes fall 20% or more from their high point. The good news is that bear markets generally last a third of the time of bull markets. The primary trend of the markets is up, just not up all of the time. In addition, up markets correct from time to time but a correction does not change the general trend of the market as a whole. Corrections are when the indexes fall less than 20%. You have to expect this kind of turbulence when you invest in stocks, but over the long term they are the best wealth builder we have.

One more caution. Invariably, you are going to talk to someone who is boasting about making a killing in the stock market. They will tell you they bought XYZ stock and sold it a month later making a bundle. You need to be highly skeptical of these kinds of claims. First of all, people only talk about their winners. You have to really push them to open up about a loser, and if they are investing in individual stocks, I can guarantee you they have some significant losers. Secondly, they most likely were using some of the techniques I listed earlier. Those techniques can be successful in the short run, but sooner or later they will cause you to lose big money. My advice, stick with the recommendations I presented in this chapter and over the long term, you will come out way ahead of the trade in and out crowd.

For fixed income investing I only gave you the choice of Short Term Corporate Bond fund. As I am writing this book, we have record low interest rates. The rates have been low for a long time but the Federal Reserve Bank has started to lift some of the measures it took to keep rates so low. When rates rise, bonds lose value. This is only important if you do not hold a bond to maturity, and instead, sell it through a broker. At maturity the issuer of the bond pays you back all of your money. Mutual Funds/ETFs, however, are priced everyday on the market value of the bonds they hold on that day. So if rates are going up, you are losing money in a bond mutual fund or ETF. Short term bonds, those with only 5 years to maturity or less, will fluctuate some, but losses will be modest. Longer term bonds, those with more than 5 years to maturity, can have substantial losses if rates continue to rise. So here is my advice. Continue to stay with short term corporate bond funds until they yield 5% or more. Right now they yield around 1%, so it may be years before they yield 5%. When that milestone is reached, begin switching your fixed income investments into a longer term fund. For longer term bonds, I prefer a Total Bond Market fund or Exchange Traded Fund. In the index, I will give you the names of my favorite intermediate term bond investments.

There is one more thing about investments I want to make you are aware of, and that is a Roth IRA. A Roth IRA was sadly not available during most of my investing career but it is the most generous, wealth building retirement account our government has ever made available to working people. You can open a Roth at any of the four brokerage companies I recommended. You can only invest money after you have paid taxes on it first, unlike a regular IRA which is funded by before tax contributions. Since you have already paid taxes on your contributions, you can take out that money at any time, but if you take out earnings on that money, you will be taxed with a 10% penalty along with regular taxes. All of the money is available to you tax free at age 59 and ½. What you can invest in is the same as for a regular IRA. Monies inside of a Roth IRA are not subject to the required-minimum-distribution rules that come into effect at age 70. Please look into the Roth IRA for all or part of your after tax savings and investments. Your broker or tax advisor can help you with more information.

Chapter 7

Earning Income

Earning a good income in many ways is the direct result of the choices you make about education and training. However, once you secure a job, you need to add your own personal effort, assertiveness, and creativity as additional factors in earning the most you can.

Earning an above average income is so critical to achieving your financial goals. So far, I have laid out a detailed plan for you. The plan requires the discipline to save money, to track your spending, to set a goal of how much you need to save to be secure or independent, and I also laid out a simple investment plan to grow your wealth. However, if you do not make enough income, none of the above is going to really work. I don't have an exact minimum you need to earn annually in order for this plan to work, but I would say you are in trouble if you are single and make below $50,000 a year. If you are a married couple, the amount needed is $60,000 or more a year. A lot depends on the cost of living where you live, and how well you can control your spending. I don't expect you to make a top salary on day one of your first job, but within a few years you need to be making close to the minimums I listed above. Moreover, the more you make, the easier it is going to be to save, and also the faster you can grow your wealth. So earning as much as you can is critical.

I want to share some observations of mine. The more hard physical labor a job requires, usually the lower the pay. It is a shame that the market place for jobs works this way, but it does. That is why people who work outside in the hot and the cold not only have exhausting jobs, but they are under-appreciated when payday rolls around. Also, any job that you can train someone to do in 30 minutes or less generally does not pay well. Retail clerks, cashiers, and fast food jobs all come to mind.

On the other hand, when you perform work people hate to do themselves, then the pay begins to rise. I could list a bunch of jobs here but I will list just a few: window washers, house cleaning, pool maintenance, roofing repair, chimney repairs, plumbing work, electrical work, and on and on. The more training it takes to do a job, the more it pays. If you need a license or certification, the pay increases more.

When you get to work that most people are incapable of doing themselves, then the pay really starts to climb. Some examples: lawyer, electrician, dentist, nurse practitioner, dermatologist (MD), software administrator for main-frame computers, civil engineer, geologist, and so on.

Another issue I want to discuss is the difference between having a hobby, and how you earn your income. A lot has been written about doing what you love in life to earn money, and then what you do for a living will never feel like work. I totally do not agree with that line of reasoning and furthermore, I feel it is leading a lot of people down the road of very low earnings for their entire working lives. Many people are good at sports, playing the guitar or piano, painting a landscape, brewing beer, but making a good living doing any of those hobbies or leisure activities is a long shot. The problem is that if you pursue a hobby as a career, it may take you many years to realize there is no real money in it, costing you dearly in quality of life and a secure financial future. Additionally, when you go from doing something you really enjoy as a hobby and then try to make it a business, you may just ruin something you used to really enjoy.

I have a solution to consider if you are drawn to something that is a hobby or sport. Don't gamble with your lively hood. Make sure you put your education and training into something that offers you a prosperous and financially secure life. In other words, pick a career, profession, or trade where you know going in there is a very high probability a job will be waiting for you when you graduate, and a job that pays above average wages. I am not asking you to work in a profession you hate. Narrow a list down to 3 good paying careers that you have an interest in. Find people who have worked in those jobs and ask them what the duties are, chances for advancement, and what you could expect to make. Do some research! Most of us only know about work that we see performed every day, but I can tell you for sure there are a lot of niche professions and trades you will never come into contact with that pay high incomes. I also have found that many people do not know what kind of work they would enjoy until they get into a company and try a couple of things. In my career, I held several positions in different departments all within the same company. I learned something important about the business in each position and the knowledge I acquired along the way was a factor in each promotion I received.

After you are settled in your career job, then look into making money on the side from your hobby. I know this is a safe approach to the hobby issue. If you feel you are outstanding at a hobby or activity, then get some expert advice before you invest too much time in it, and test the waters on a part time basis. Remember, time is money, and you do not have any time to waste on a wrong choice.

Below, I have listed my top 5 college degrees where I feel there is a good chance of finding a high paying job shortly after getting your degree. Here they are:

1. **Computer Science**
   Every business, every hospital, every city, county, state, needs highly trained computer people. There are many jobs in computers and they pay well. There are also many areas of specialty in a computer science program. We all know programmers are the key to making software do the wonderful things it does. There are jobs writing software at Microsoft, Twitter, Apple, IBM, Google, and many more mid to small size companies. Another area of specialty is data base administrators on mainframe systems. There are computer safety people. Hacking and theft of data are a huge societal problem. You need to specialize in one of several computer areas to make the most money the professions offers.
   Drawbacks: You have to like computers and working by yourself. Most workers in this field work a lot of hours. You have to continually train and take

courses or you may find yourself obsolete. There tend to be a lot of crisis and deadlines that come with computer work. Also, outsourcing is a constant worry along with immigrant workers who will work for lower wages.

2. **Accounting or Financial Analyst**
Just like computer jobs, all businesses and government entities have accountants on their staff. There are many specialty areas in accounting, such as: auditor, internal auditor, tax accountant, forensic accountant, financial analyst, controller, and more. Accounting departments and computer departments work closely together on a lot of projects. Accountants usually report to the senior management of the company and often take over leadership positions in many organizations.
Drawbacks: You have to pass the CPA exam to earn the top salaries. Most jobs require knowing a lot about several accounting software systems. Accountants also work long hours and face deadlines quite often. Many menial accounting jobs have been eliminated by computer programs but the accountants that are left have more responsible positions and status within their organizations.

3. **Engineering Degree**

There are at least 20 different types of engineering degrees you can get and the work can be dramatically varied. Here are some types of engineers: civil engineers, mechanical engineers, petroleum engineers, chemical engineer, electrical engineers, mining engineers, and several more. These degrees require a lot of math and science. Engineering jobs pay high starting salaries and being an engineer is a high status job in most companies.

Drawbacks: You have to like math and science. Most college programs take 5 years to get your degree. Although starting salaries are high, engineering salaries seem to top out sooner than other professions. There is always the problem of too much experience in a narrow area or process that is not transferable to another job in your field.

4. **Registered Nurse and Nurse Practitioner**

Nursing is a varied and people oriented career. There are many specialty areas within a nursing program, such as: operating room nurse, pre-natal nurse, post operating room nurse, occupational nurse, nurse anesthesiologist, and more. Best of all there are a lot of jobs available in nursing. You can make more money by becoming a nurse practitioner and the jobs for practitioners are growing rapidly.

Drawbacks: You have to like a lot of people contact. Nurses work all hours including shift work. The doctors get all the glory and usually call all of the shots in medicine. It can be very stressful work and you are on your feet a lot. There can also be competition from immigrants at lower salaries.

5. **Education Degrees**

There are schools everywhere and they all have a lot of teachers in them. There is a variety of subjects to teach and some subjects have a lot more jobs available. Teaching can be a stepping stone into assistant principal job, or principal, administrator, superintendent. Most states have a lot of school districts and each one of them has a superintendent and other highly paid administrators. Most of our cities also have community college systems that also hire a lot of teachers. Retirement programs are usually outstanding.

Drawbacks: In order to make good money, you have to have a master's degree. The sooner you get your masters the better. Teaching is no longer a safe career. Teachers are more frequently being let go for a number of reasons. Parents can be totally unreasonable and problematic. Students can be hostile and violent sometimes.

All of my top 5 degrees offer a lot of jobs and for the most part, you do not have to worry about your job being outsourced to another country. Another positive for these careers is that you can count on steady employment throughout your life. Remember, all jobs/professions have drawbacks, so do not be deterred in what you want to do by a few negatives.

There are several other degree programs I like but they do not have the depth of ready jobs that my top 5 have.

Here are a few of my other top picks: geology, pharmacy, business degrees (many areas of specialty), chemistry, math, biology, statistics, actuary, law enforcement, and government administrators.

Remember this is about earning money and getting a job after you graduate as soon as possible. Here is a short list of my avoid degrees: history, English, sociology, pre-law, liberal arts, literature, art, graphic art, architecture, anthropology, and more. Some of these degree programs do have jobs available, especially in teaching at the college level. If you set out in the beginning to teach at the college level and you are willing to put in the time, money, and sacrifice for a doctorate, then several of these degree programs have the potential for a well paying long term career. I do not want to discourage you if one of these areas of study is your preferred choice. Just make sure you know in advance what the job and income opportunities are, and maybe there is a way to incorporate these subjects in your life as a hobby rather than a profession.

There are also a number of trades that I like very much. Many of these trades have a lot of jobs available and the pay is good. There are also many business opportunities in the trades as well. I highly recommend getting formal training, preferably an Associate's degree at a minimum. Here is my top 5 list: plumbing, electrician, welder, dental hygienist, and carpenter/general contractor. There are many more trades to consider, and there are a few that I would avoid. Here are a few avoids: culinary, chimney sweeps, secretarial training, janitorial, barber, and more. You have to look at potential earnings and the number of jobs available. For instance, there are a lot of culinary jobs but the pay is horrible and the hours are very demanding. Just do your homework by talking to people who do these trades before you commit to an education program.

I like master's degrees. Anyone with a bachelor's degree should be considering a master's, however you need to weigh what it cost to get a master's and decide if it will boost your earnings or your career. There are some combinations of bachelor's and master's degrees that are particularly in demand. For example, a degree in accounting with a master's in computer science, or the other way around. An engineering degree paired with a master's of business administration or MBA. Also an engineering degree with a master's in computer science. Talk to people in your field about master's program that will compliment your bachelor's degree.

However, before I would work on a master's degree, I would first see if there is a certification you can get in your field. Certifications can sometimes give your earnings an instant increase, and they may put you in a good position for a promotion down the road. I have already mentioned the value of Certified Public Accountant or CPA. I got a couple of certifications myself, Certified Financial Planner, and Certified Fund Specialist. Before I got my certifications, I did a little research and I was amazed at how many there are available. When you see initials on a business card after a person's name, many times those are certifications. Ask people in your field what is a highly valued certification, or where you work, find out what your company considers valuable. Do a little homework and then get started in the evenings and weekends on having at least one certification.

By the way, you can have too many. Two are just about right. In my opinion, they lose value if you have too many.

This brings me to two Larry's rules:

10. **Deciding how you will make a living is one of the most important decisions you will make in life. Before you choose, look for job availability, an above average salary, and investigate to see if you can expect to be employed your whole working life.**

11. **Most hobbies, sports, and crafts, have a low probability as a successful, high paying career. Instead, pick a proven career or trade to earn a living, and enjoy the other in your spare time for fun.**

I have approached this subject as though you have just finished high school and have everything in front of you to choose from. However, if you are already working and not earning up to your potential, then start over. Plan your escape from a dead end profession or trade. Take courses at night, during the weekend, or by correspondence over the internet. Do not quit what you are doing until you have finished your studies and have a job waiting for you. If you have a spouse whose job pays all of the bills, then you have the luxury of full time pursuing your new endeavor.

Another avenue for bringing in income is starting or owning a business. I think there two situations to consider. Wait to start a business until you have reached financial security. Having substantial savings makes everything easier and more secure. Or, when you first get out of college and have nothing to lose. Either way, starting a business or buying a business is a high risk, high reward way to go. Most small businesses fail during the first 5 years, but when you hit something that works, the payoff can be surprisingly good. You also have to know if running a business is for you. Not everyone is suited to running a business. Read, study, and be an expert before you jump in. Also try a business idea during your off hours first before quitting your day job. If it does not work out, get back to your money making career as soon as possible.

In my way of thinking, even employees should consider themselves business owners. The business is you. You just have one customer. It is your job to keep your customer happy and satisfied, and to also get as much revenue out of your customer as you can. Like any good business owner, you need to manage your customer's perception of you, and keep your plans, your personal life, and your opinions to yourself. Running a business is all about the customer.

When I first went to work after finishing college, I noticed the bosses at every level above me had more control over their time, they didn't work any more hours than I did, but they got paid a whole lot more. In fact the region manager, who was the top boss where I first worked, often took 2 hour lunches, flew off to have meetings with his boss and customers occasionally, and spent a whole lot of time just chatting in his office. It became clear to me that climbing the ladder was not only the way to make more money but also the way to have a more enjoyable work life.

From then on, I made it a priority to climb that ladder. I set out to find what it took to get the next spot above me. I discovered that one of the most important things I could do was to just ask for a promotion, and keep asking. If climbing the ladder is important to you, make sure your boss and his or her boss knows you are willing to do whatever it takes to get ahead.

In my mid 30's I read a magazine article about the difficulty people over 50 were having in getting jobs. I looked around at my company, which employed close to 250 people, and I noticed that there were only 3 employees over 50 years of age in the whole company! Furthermore, I noticed that employees, after they turned 50, for one reason or another, were gone before they reached age 55. This was a big eye opener for me and caused me to make a big change in my long term plans. I liked what I was doing at that time and I made an above average salary, so I wanted to continue there as long as I could. This realization led me to really seriously begin building my net worth the way I am recommending in this book, and my goal was to be totally financially independent by the time I was age 50, so no matter what happened, my wife and I would be secure.

In addition, I decided to have a back-up career in case I was let go unexpectedly. That is when I started taking classes at night to prepare for a financial planning career, hoping I never needed to use it. Of course, I did not discuss my observations or plans with anyone other than my wife. Even after I passed the CFP exam a few years later, I cautiously let my bosses know, but by that time I had been promoted and the CFP training ended up helping me tremendously in my new position.

My advice to you is to be prepared. Keep your resume up to date, work on that master's degree or certification, and be thinking about what you would do if lightning strikes and you find yourself without a job. More importantly, follow the steps in this book and build a financial firewall around you and your family. Have the financial where-with-all to weather the storm. As you get older and your pay increases, you become very vulnerable to having your career unexpectedly interrupted.

Today it is very common for employees over 50 to be the first to be let go in a cost cutting move, merger, re-organization, consolidation, etc. Don't expect age discrimination laws to protect you. There are a so many loop holes in the law it is almost impossible to get a ruling in your favor and it takes years to get your day in court. Put your safety and well being into your own hands and follow my financial plan.

Chapter 8

Spending

This is the one area of your life where you have 100% control. I want you to avoid being a spend-every-penny person, but on the other hand, I want you to not deny yourself too many things, because we never know how long we are going to live. I hope to help you strike the right balance for yourself.

There is one publication I want you to go down to your local library and get in the habit of reading each month, and that is Consumer Reports. There is no better objective source of consumer information in our society. They do thorough work, and they ignore brands, labels, and how much things cost. You have to read it regularly because they randomly investigate different products so you never know what is coming next. Over the years they have torn into toothpaste, hand lotion, polo shirts, toasters, cell phones, just about every consumer item you can think of.

I love their methodology for finding what is best on the market. Among the many tests they perform, they have people blindly try out items so they have no idea who made it, or what it cost, and then they ask them to rate it after a considerable testing time. What is apparent after reading the reviews over a long period of time is that the most expensive item is rarely the best. In fact, quite often the most expensive product is near the very bottom of the list. So equating price with quality is not a good way to judge what to buy. I want you to have the best information before you spend your hard earned money.

I also want to point out to you that in general, the more heavily products or services are advertised the more profitable they are to the company selling the item. Advertising on T.V. for instance, is very expensive and you have to recover that cost in the price of a product, plus make a good profit. That is why we see pharmaceuticals advertised over and over again, even though a doctor has to write you a prescription for you to buy the product!

The money that you spend represents your life. I always think about how long I have to work to pay for something. If you are paid $15 per hour, then how many hours of your life do you have to toil to pay for things you really do not need. A cell phone that cost $250, takes nearly 17 hours or two days of work. A big screen T.V. that cost $800 takes over 53 hours of your hard work. All those clothes in your closet that you never wear, they represent more than just wasted money. Just think about how many hours you have to work before you open your wallet to buy something that is not really necessary.

In America, there is no limit to how much you can spend on items you want. What I am trying to say is that if you want to try to imitate the rich and famous, there is someone out there who will help you and will take your money. In almost every category of spending I am going to cover, you can have items custom made, gold plated, custom painted, custom designed, imported, and on and on. Watching the

Home and Garden Channel, I am amazed at the ways that home owners can find to needlessly spend money. A few years ago I watched a segment where a lady asked a landscaping company to turn her back yard into a professional water park! Her budget, all coming from a home equity loan, was over the top. Today, she now has a house where the value is considerably less, but she still has the huge home equity debt to pay back, and the back yard water park cost a fortune to maintain and keep up. She did not take into account that there are park district swimming pools everywhere in America, and you only have to pay when you actually use them.

One other concept should always be on your mind when you are about to spend money: Is the item you are buying a need or a want. By need, I mean something you have to have in order for your life to function. If not, it is a want. For instance, you need a basic car to get to work and run errands, but if you decide to buy a gas guzzling, expensive SUV then you took something you need and turned it into a totally unnecessary want. Keep your wants list short and under control, but never forgo something that you have to have to live.

I am starting with the most expensive things you buy and working my way down. If you get the most expensive things wrong, there is no way you can save enough on smaller items to ever make up for a big item mistake. This list is only a sampling of the things most people buy.

1. Housing

You have to get this one right, or it will undermine everything else you are trying to do to build net worth. First of all, there is nothing wrong with renting for a while. My test for buying property is: do not buy unless you are absolutely sure you will live there for a minimum of 5 years. It takes that long to have even a chance of covering the selling cost of your house when you sell. So, if you have a chance of being transferred soon or you already dislike your job and cannot see yourself being there for 5 years, then rent. If you rent, you want to pay as little rent as possible, so no renting rooms that you do not use or need. It is not your property. You are just paying to use it for a short period of time. If your rent is low, you can save more for a down payment on a property that will be all yours later.

In my opinion, location is the most important factor to consider in a place to live. You go to work 5 days a week or maybe 6 days. That is 40 trips there and back each month, or more. Plus the wear and tear you put on a car, which is your next most expensive item to buy. Not to mention the gasoline. So, I would not choose a place to live that is further than a 30 minute drive from where you work.

If you work a lot of hours, travel a lot, really do not like yard work, or have a busy social life, consider a townhouse or condo. Some people feel that the association dues for condos and townhouses cost too much, but the associations are just reserving money a little each month for repairs and maintenance. House owners spend the same amount on maintaining their property, but because the expense is paid only when they repair or replace something, they feel it cost less over time. It does not cost less.

Buy only what you know you will need and use daily. If a house with 3 bedrooms, a 2 car garage, of average size meets your needs, do not buy more. If a one bedroom condo with one covered parking space meets your requirements, buy no more. This is not about keeping up with the Joneses or fulfilling your fantasies (man caves, movie rooms, swimming pools, etc.). I have seen so many house-poor people who have to limit everything else in their lives to afford a rambling, oversized house. After they buy it, they have to furnish it, pay property taxes, heat and cool it. The expense never stops. Just be realistic and give it a lot of thought and by all means, make sure your home purchase does not jeopardize your 20% a year savings goal.

Having to put your house, town house, or condo up for sale is one of the most expensive things you can do. You are going to give up 6% of the total value of your property to a real estate sales company plus you have to pay another 6% that is imbedded in the price of the new property you are buying. You have to pay movers, attorneys to review the contract,

95

appraisers, surveyors, title insurance, and also for a closing agent. If you can buy a place that you will be in until you retire, that would be the best net worth builder you could do for yourself. However, sometimes you just have to move. I did.

A house is not an investment. It does not earn income and it cost a lot of money to maintain it. Houses do appreciate but long term studies have found that houses appreciate only at about the inflation rate. House prices went crazy for a few years from 2002 to 2007, but that was a rare exception and you will most likely not see that again in your life time. So, buy a home to live in, to enjoy, and to eventually own without a mortgage so you have a place to live for the rest of your life.

When it comes to financing a house, if you are in your 20's, a 30 year fixed rate mortgage makes some sense, especially until you have time put into your career and you are earning more. However, your goal is to pay off that debt as soon as you can and way before 30 years. I want you to keep your priorities straight, so paying down mortgage debt early should never interfere with your 20% savings each month. If you are older or find yourself earning more sooner than you thought, go for a 15 year mortgage when you buy. Also, if you refinance to get a better rate, move to a shorter term mortgage as well.

Here is another Larry's Rule

12. **Owning a debt free place to live in is a key part of your financial goals. Pay off your mortgage as soon as you can, but never interrupt your 20% savings you put away each month.**

2. Automobiles

At its basic level, a car is for your transportation. If you try to communicate anything else, such as the type of car you own is who you are, or how much your car cost and what that says about you, then you are wasting money.

As I mentioned earlier, your first car or two you will need to finance but I want you to move to paying cash for your cars as soon as you comfortably can. My strategy is to start off buying used cars and financing them for 30 months or less. Once you have paid off the debt, keep making the car payment but put it into a reserve for your next car. If you can drive that first car for say 5 years or longer, you will have a larger down payment on the second used car and a trade-in. Hopefully you can finance the next car for an even shorter period, and repeat the process, until you have enough money in your reserve and with your trade-in to pay cash.

Using Consumer Reports is crucial in buying a new or used car. They will give you guidance about which cars last and require the fewest repairs. I have my favorites and I feel they are a good choice whether you are buying used or new: Honda Civic, Toyota Corolla, Hyundai Elantra, Kia Rio, Nissan Sentra, Honda CVR, Toyota Prius, Ford Focus Hybrid, to name a few. I want a car that is comfortable, uses little gasoline, and has enough power to take me on a long trip. I like power windows, but I do not have to have every gadget known to man.

You have to shop for cars and I like going to dealers that have been in the community for a time. I also like hearing other people's experience at dealers. Take your time, don't be pushed by a salesman, and ask for everything. Most libraries have books that are printed each month on car prices. Look for Black Book, NADA Guide, or Kelley Blue Book. If you are buying used, you may also want to do a title search. You can order them on- line.

A car is a big purchase, and to get the most for your money you have to drive a car for years. When it comes to new cars, expect to drive it 8 to 10 years minimum. A used car will hopefully last 6 to 8 years. Take care of your car. Follow the manual for oil changes, air filters, timing belts, transmission flush, and more. You need that car to go when you turn the key on.

Do not lease your car. Leasing ensures that you will never live without a car payment. Before you go to the dealer to buy your car, go to your bank and apply for a car loan. Banks offer better rates most of the time and it will help you build your credit rating with them. Do not tell the dealer who you will be financing with until you have picked out a car and have agreed on a price. Dealers make money financing cars and they will do everything they can to get you to finance it through them.

3. **Motorcycles, Motor Boats, Sail Boats, Motor Homes, Snow Mobiles**

I have had friends who got the bug to own one or more of these big ticket items and it is a disease that is not easily cured. For the average person, any of these can be a long term wealth destroyer. Not only are all of these items expensive to buy, to store, to license, and insure, but they are seldom used! During your peak earning years, age 30 to 50, you can expect to work 50 hours a week. That simply does not leave you enough leisure time to use these vehicles enough to justify the huge up-front cost. And to make matters worse, most people buy a boat, a motor home, etc., and then before long, they want a larger one. I see unused vehicles like these parked in garages, drive ways, storage lots, all of over the U.S. just waiting for a day they are actually used.

All of these items depreciate quickly and the resale market is not good. My advice, if you feel you have to own one of these items, buy a used one so you can skip all of that costly first year depreciation. Or I have even a better suggestion. You can rent all of these for a reasonable cost for the short periods of time that you actually use them. Even better still, spend your spare time with your friends and family going for a walk, a hike, a bicycle ride, and many more activities that are for the most part, free!

4. Furniture

I really enjoyed a house full of comfortable and attractive furniture. I want my house to feel like a home, but I still want good value. You can find really good used wooden furniture in resale shops, garage sales, estates sales, and flea markets at a fraction of the cost of new. I think it makes sense to buy some of your wooden furniture used.

However, I like to buy upholstered furniture new. You can also find a lot of used upholstered furniture but usually the springs and cushions are practically worn out from use, and the fabric is in rough shape. You can have furniture re-covered and cushions re-stuffed, but my experience is that the renovation cost is about the same as just buying new upholstered pieces, and I would rather have new.

5. Food

I believe in eating fresh, quality food. I do not want you to skimp here, but you need to be on guard for some pitfalls that are easy to fall into. The easier it is to just take food home, warm it up in the micro-wave or oven, and serve, the more it cost and the more likely it is not to be near as healthy. The best quality food is food that you prepare yourself from scratch. I find the pre prepared stuff is full of salt, sugar, and fat. I call those the 3 addictives! The more of your grocery spending you do in the produce department, the healthier your food is going to be. A diet that is loaded with fruit and vegetables is the best way to go.

Before you do your grocery shopping, have a plan of what you are going to prepare everyday of the week. Shop from a list and avoid the impulse stuff you trip over in the store aisles. Find a grocery store nearby that has consistently low prices and good quality. Leave the fancy stores that are full of take-out foods to the trendy crowd.

Eating out will also cut a big hole in your spending plans. That does not mean that you should never eat out, just set reasonable goals for yourself. Try to limit yourself to places that are a good value and where you do not have to tip. I especially like Panera Bread, the Corner Bakery, Jason's Deli, and other similar places where you get good quality food at a reasonable price, and no tipping. I think once a week eating out journey is a reasonable limit, especially while you are trying to get your financial life up and going, and on track with your goals. The important thing is to stay out of the high priced, sit down restaurants. Eating out is another one of the areas where there is no limit to what you can spend.

One other way I save money eating out is by drinking water with all my meals. I drink water at home so eating out is no different. Drinks are the major profit center for restaurants and they really push up the cost of a meal. If you want to drink wine or beer, have a glass at home after you get home. A glass or two of wine during a meal out will double the amount of your bill. Even better, just forget the wine and beer altogether! It is expensive, full of yeast and mold, and any benefit is heavily out-weighed by the negatives.

6. Clothing

No one knows where you bought your clothes unless a company logo is on it. So stay with moderate priced clothes and remember Consumer Reports shows that high price has no correlation with quality. I try to wear solid color polo shirts, and I limit my pants colors to khaki, and black so I have many combinations that work together. I also wear a lot of knit shirts that do not have to go to the cleaners. I have a Kohl's credit card and they send me a steady stream of discounts that make shopping fun. When I get a 30% discount card that is when I do my serious shopping. I usually get 30% off 2 or 3 times a year. I also buy some clothes at Amazon, especially when I am sure of the sizes. Amazon allows me to jump to a little higher quality sometimes, and still stay within my budget.

I also have an outlet mall close by and I check them out for good deals. I find my best deals there near the end of the season. So I look for winter clothes in January or February, and summer clothes in July or August.

One money drain with clothes is buying things you never wear and buying too many similar things. It is hard to go through life without buying a thing or two you never wear, but once you find out what you really like to wear, stay with it for as longs as you can. Also, if something is in your closet that you have not worn in the last 12 months, out it goes.

7. Shoes

Most people have way too many shoes in the closet. Not only does it take a big closet to keep them in, but there is a lot of money tied up in shoes. My advice is never duplicate things you already have.

To make my shoes last longer, I use foot powder in them every day. I wear predominantly casual shoes so all I do is wipe them down with a wet cloth every now and then. I buy my shoes at the outlet center and sometimes on Amazon.

8. Sheets and Towels

Keep it simple and buy all of your sheets and towels in white. I like color in a house, just put your color in other items. If you go with all white, you can find it everywhere and it is easy to wash since you can throw everything together. You will have more choices in white as well. Again, keep it simple.

9. Staying Fit

Keeping fit can lead you into a real mess of fees, contracts, and extra charges that take a long time to undo. You do not have to have an expensive health club membership to keep in shape. For many years I have had a stationary bike and a padded mat in my basement. Buy a book on exercise so you can put together a workout routine and you will save a bunch of money. In addition to my basement workout, I walk a couple of miles 5 days a week.

If you want a health club experience, see if your park district has a facility. Some park districts have all of the latest equipment, classes, and sometimes indoor tennis courts, racket ball, swimming pools, and more. Never sign a health club contract on the spot. Take it home and read it first. Make sure you can get out of that contract and never commit to more than 12 months.

10. Education Expense

College costs have gone to the moon. There are some savings out there, however. I am a big proponent of spending your first two years of college at a community college. Just make sure the courses you take are accepted where you intend to finish. Hiring managers want to know where you got your degree, not where you started college. In my area, the local community college estimates a full time student will spend about $3,500 per year, and to that you have to add some transportation cost and books. The state university charges $18,000 a year and that is before you pay for room and board, and books. Private schools are way more expensive.

Set a goal to not go into debt the first two years of college by using your community colleges. And please do not feel going to a community college is your lesser choice. At a community college, it is up to you to make your college experience memorable. Be active on campus, join clubs, go to hear guest lectures, and concerts. Do not just go to class and race out of there.

For your last two years, pick a school that is known for the field you plan to go into. Recruiters are going to target the schools that are known for engineers, accountants, educators, nurses, computer science majors, etc. In other words, finish your degree where you can get the best education for the money you spend.

For graduate school, I am leaning towards taking classes on-line. Today many of the top state schools offer masters programs where you attend the lectures on-line. You take your test at testing centers. A lot of graduate students never set foot on the campus or if they do, it is for classes where there is lab work or some other course that requires special facilities. Living in your own home and working while you learn at night is very attractive and cost effective.

If you have to borrow for your education, get a Federal government sponsored loan. Government loans give you some protections that other lenders do not offer. Once you have graduated, if you can comfortably make the payments do not be in a hurry to pay off your education loan. Especially if you are able to make the payments and still save 20% of your income as I have outlined in this book. Usually government college loans carry low interest rates and if you pay them on time, they help you establish credit. Just try to borrow as little as you possibly can.

11. Leisure Activities

The first leisure activity I want to mention is casino gambling. Many people in America consider this their past time. Casinos operate on a foundation of mathematics. You can only be ahead in all of the games they offer, temporarily. If they can get you to stay, the math guarantees they will win in the end. My advice, find something else to do rather than give your hard earned money away.

The Lottery is even worse. The odds are so bad they almost guarantee that you could play every week for the rest of your life and never be a winner. Gambling of any sort is just not consistent with building a sizeable net worth in your life time.

Shopping is another leisure activity that can be so destructive to your financial life. We all have to shop for the things we need. You need to compare prices and brands, and there is no substitute for trying clothes on first or making sure shoes fit. What I am talking about here is shopping to fill time, because you are bored, or to escape loneliness. Shopping can become an addiction and like all addictions, it starts by doing it over and over again. Unless you actually need something, my advice, stay out of stores.

Another big money eater is travel, especially foreign travel. I have done some foreign travel and I learned a ton and enjoyed it immensely. However, I waited to do my foreign travel until I could pay cash for everything and until after I had accomplished my long term financial goals. Before that, my wife and I took trips in the U.S. where we could stay with relatives, or just long weekend trips, and we kept the cost very low. Don't let travel get you off track with your goals.

One more big money drain is attending professional sports events. Professional sports cost a bundle to attend. Try to follow your team on T.V, and rather than watch sports, get out and participate in a sport.

12. Electronics

For many people, when you add up cable TV, home phone, cell phone, internet service, and maybe a streaming service, it is their largest monthly expense. Almost all of these fall in the "want" category, except for basic telephone service.

Cable TV is very expensive and confusing. I have friends who have put up an antenna and canceled their cable service. They get about 20 stations all for free! The best value with cable T.V. companies is a package I call expanded basic but over time the fees seem to just go up and up. You have to change service providers periodically to get a lower price.

Many people who have cell phones go ahead and cancel their land line. To save money on my cell phone and service I bought a refurbished phone on Amazon and paid cash for it. I went with a service provider where you can order just what you want on a month to month basis. My provider is Consumer Cellular. That was the best value I could find. Another low cost provider is Republic Wireless.

For Internet service, many people I know switch service providers periodically when specials discounts are offered. They buy a router/modem for each service making it easier to switch. Basically, with all of these electronics you have to do a little work to find the best combination of low cost and good service.

Those are the major items I wanted to cover. Overall, do what is practical and necessary to live. Live simply, frugally, and with purpose. Until you reach your savings goals you should be on a mission to make the financial security finish line. Obviously, there are many more areas of spending we encounter and you will have to use your own sense of doing what is best for yourself for the least amount of money.

Can you take saving money too far? Absolutely! Please promise me you will never count how many sheets of toilet paper members of your family use, or scream at everyone who leaves a light on in a room, or everyone who holds the refrigerator door open too long, or buys some clothing item they never wear, or keep the thermostat set to freezing during winter or too hot during summer, and more.

You can go from being frugal to being a miserable, tyrant miser very fast. They best way to get your loved ones on board with being frugal is to model the behaviors you want them to adopt. However, we all know that may not work so please try to find some balance in getting everyone on board. Try trade-offs, such as I will do this if you do that. In the end, let all of your family members choose for themselves what is appropriate within limits.

Here is another Larry's rule:

13. Being frugal is good, being a miser is intolerable. Treat all of your family members with love and acceptance, even if they do not share your goals.

Chapter 9

Time

So far, I have covered 3 important variables in your planning that you either have some, or complete control over. Here is the list:

1. Earning a good steady income
2. Rate of return on your investments, with reasonable risk
3. Spending, or how cheaply can you live

There is a 4th variable and that is time. And that leads me to a Larry's Rule.

13. Start your wealth building plans as soon as you possibly can. Having a longer time to save, means you can build larger wealth and also have a lower monthly savings goal.

Getting started early with saving money is so important. An early start will give you a much larger net worth at the end. Let's look at some examples.

If you are fortunate to start saving money at age 24, and you save only $300 per month, let's see how much you will have at age 60, with a 6% return over those 36 years. My calculations show you will have a nest egg of approximately $458,000.

Let's take another person who does not get started with saving money until age 35, but they are able to save $600 per month. At age 60 that person will have $416,000. So even by saving twice as much per month, the 35 year old saver ends up with less money than our 24 year old early saver. It takes time for the power of compound returns to really work for you.

Let's take these examples further. Our 24 year old saver figures out that he or she will need $650,000 to reach financial independence, and they target age 55 for their goal. To attain that goal, they will have to save $603 per month for 31 years. Now, we will keep the same end goal of $650,000 at age 55 but the saving starts at age 34. This saver will have to save $1,293 per month to reach the same goal. That means it will take our older saver a little more than twice the monthly savings, to reach the same goal.

As I have related to you, I did not have well defined financial goals the first 7 years of my working life after graduating from college. Instead of focusing on financial security and saving money, I was buying larger and larger houses. However, buying larger houses was not a complete waste because I did come away with some appreciation and equity. I did save money, just not near as much as I could have had I been focused on building my net worth and achieving financial security. At age 35 I finally gained the knowledge to start focusing on my own financial goals. But I had to save much higher amounts to make it happen in a reasonable time.

Today many people see the only long term financial goal they really have as retirement, and sadly, they don't plan to even think about retirement until after age 40. As you can see by my examples, by age 40 you may not be able to save the large monthly amounts needed to retire! Let's put some numbers together and see what it takes.

So far my examples have been of a single person in their 20's. Let's now look at a married couple at age 40 who wants financial independence at age 55. Their spreadsheet shows an average monthly expense of $4,100 but it includes their house payment of $1,800 per month and a car payment of $420 per month. They intend to pay off the car but the house payment will not be paid off until they are age 60, so it stays. Their adjusted monthly expense is $3,680 (after the car is paid off) and their yearly expenses are $44,160 ($3,680 X 12). If we divide $44,160 by .06, the investment amount needed in savings is $736,000, and I am going to add $100,000 to the investment amount to cover inflation, replacing cars, house maintenance, etc. With 15 years to go and using a 6% investment return, they will need to save $2,875 per month in order to have an investment pool of $836,000 at age 55.

They have two ways they can save for this goal. One way is to live on one salary and save the other if they both work. Both spouses would continue to put 10% in their 401K at work which would cover part of the savings they need. If the lower paid spouse has a salary of $45,000 per year, then after taxes and including 10% taken out at work, they should be able to save the $2,875. Another way is for both spouses to put approximately $1,500 per month in savings with a combination of 10% at work, the rest into a joint account each month, or some other combination that equals $2,875. It can be done, but they have to both be working and both making a good income to make it happen. That is not possible for a lot of couples.

In addition, this couple will have retirement already covered after achieving their financial independence goal. At age 60 they will pay off their house mortgage, cutting their monthly expenses by another $1,800 per month. And then at any time after age 62, they could take social security but they could easily wait until age 67 and get the full amount of social security.

For most people, the very earliest age they can possibly start saving is age 25. If you go back to school for an advanced degree, or just need more time for a number of reasons, you could easily not start saving until age 30. In some fields of work you are going to have a challenge to keep working past age 55, and in other professions, working to age 65 is common. Even if you lose your primary career at age 55, you can still find work but probably not making the top salary you were making before. Will you have the savings and investments necessary to support yourself throughout your life?

Chapter 10

Action!

Get going! Start your financial plan today by just asking for a receipt every time you spend money. Get a note book and start recording all of those receipts every day. Just doing this much takes almost no effort and gets you started. Then spend a little time setting up your spreadsheet. Please, copy mine and just make the minor adjustments in categories that better fit your spending. If you do just this much, it will get you out of the dark of not knowing how much you spend each month, where it is all going, and whether you are spending more than you make.

Do not put this book away and just tell yourself that someday later you want to get started building your wealth. There is no time to waste. Having a lot of time ahead of you is one of the greatest assets you have in reaching financial security, even if you never make the kind of money you hope to make! As I have already shown you, having a lot of time means you can reach your goals with a lower monthly savings amount.

There really is no good alternative to following this plan that I have laid out for you. No one is going to knock on your door at age 50, or 60, and bail you out when you are floundering with no money in the bank and your opportunity to earn good money is near an end. At age 50 or older, you no longer will have parents or relatives willing to come to your rescue. Yes, you can still get a low wage job at just about any age but is that what you want for yourself? Poverty? It just doesn't have to be that way. You no longer have an excuse for not putting yourself in good financial shape during your adult life. You have the information and the know-how, all you need to do is execute!

I have run into some people who have rejected my proven method, saying they are going to make a whole lot of money so they feel they really do not have to plan or save money. That kind of thinking is the road to ruin and here is why. Most people who make more and more money just ratchet up their life-style as they go along. There is no limit to how much you can spend even if you make a ton of money. Without good records as to how much you are spending or how much net worth you need to keep the rich life-style going, you are destined to fail. There is no substitute for living well below your income, saving and investing the difference, and having definite savings goals you want to achieve. How many sports celebrities, music stars, TV personalities have ended up filing bankruptcy even though they make huge incomes. It happens all of the time.

The other issue with planning to make a lot of money is that it may never happen. Sometimes careers and promotions just never come to fruition. Ever notice how many Baby Boomers have had their jobs terminated after they turn age 50. Even with a lot of education and experience, many of these boomers just cannot get back into a well paying job. For many the job loss happened in what they hoped would be their highest earning years, when they planned to really knuckle down and save a bundle for retirement and security. They waited too long to start!

Remember when everyone was trying to start an internet company back in 1999, or they were going to be a home builder in 2006. Even just buying houses, fixing them up and flipping them in a short period of time seemed to be the way to wealth but it did not last very long. In all of these endeavors, there were a small number of people who got in first and got out before the market fell, and I emphasize small number. Many just got crushed with houses built and for sale, but no buyers, or with remodeled houses that would not flip, and internet dreams that never got off the ground when the money dried up.

When it comes to making money there is no sure thing. I encourage everyone to do their homework and make sure they are not starting a business near the end of a bubble or end of a trend. And never bet the ranch on a business venture. If something goes wrong, you still have a long life ahead of you. Have enough left in savings and investments to pick up the pieces and get back to work on your goals. Remember, you need enough money to support you and maybe a spouse into your 90's! If you retire at age 62, either voluntarily or involuntarily, you could easily have 30 years or more ahead of you to support yourself.

Your grandparents did not have to save big mountains of cash to retire. The World War Two generation was fortunate to have pensions offered by almost all of the major corporations. For my parents and most of our neighbors, they could count on long term employment with the same company, and all you needed to get that good job was a high school education. Unions were much more common and were a major factor in increasing salaries. Many workers during this time were trained by their company (at no cost to the worker) and the company was more likely to promote from within.

I am a Baby Boomer, and most of my friends got their college degrees in the 1960s and 70's. My college tuition was $200 a semester no matter how many courses I took, and room and board in an on-campus dorm was $900 for the whole school year! I paid for nearly half of my college expenses just working a full time summer job. I have spoken with many people who went to colleges in other states during this same period and their expenses were similar to mine or even less. Others I know went to college on the G.I. bill during this time and the government paid for just about everything! Having college debt after getting your degree was rare in this period. It was primarily graduate students who had to borrow to complete a masters or a doctorate.

That whole system of long term employment with one employer my parents enjoyed, and very low college education expense I benefitted from, began to crumble in the 1970's, and by the 1980's, it was on the way out. American businesses began to face stiff foreign competition in car manufacturing, cameras, toys, and a host of other goods during the 1970's and after. The post World War II era was over.

In the early 1980's the 401K savings plan came into being and was quickly adopted by American businesses. By the early 1990s the pensions, also called defined benefit plans, were being cancelled, and by the end of that decade, the cancellations grew in numbers. Today pensions are almost entirely gone in private business. Government workers and teachers still have them but in most states they are seriously underfunded, and changes are inevitable.

So here we are today with the working world changing dramatically. Your chances for success are entirely dependent on the choices you make. No pension plan at work? Then you have to create one for yourself, and I have given you a step by step guide on how to do that. Choose the wrong college major and you will have a hard time launching your career and earning a decent income. Spend every penny you make, and you will live your life on the edge of financial failure. In every instance there is a solution and a path to security, independence and possibly wealth.

In the index I have made a list of the books that inspired me to get on the right path. I hope you will continue your journey to financial success by reading several of the books on my list. As I said earlier, get going!

Index

Larry's Rules:

1. Your lifetime, primary financial goal is to build net worth.

2. Debt is the exact opposite of building net worth. Never go into debt unless you have no other choice.

3. Your first long term goal for building net worth is to attain financial security. Financial security is the amount of investments you need in order to generate enough income to live without working for a short period of time (4 to 8 months).

4. Track your spending and income every month, and total it for the year, hopefully forever, but for sure until you reach your goals. You need to know whether you reached your savings goal for the month, and more importantly for the year.

5. If you have a 401K or 403B retirement savings plan available at work, put 10% of your salary into it on day one or increase your contribution to 10% ASAP. No more, no less. If there is no plan at work, then open an Individual Retirement Account (IRA) for yourself and put 10% away.

6. Never take money out your retirement plans before you are age 59 and a half.

7. Your minimum savings goal including retirement savings is 20% of your gross salary each year.

8. Periodically review the list of benefits that come from achieving financial security.

9. Invest in Exchange Traded Funds or Mutual Funds that cover 5 or 6 broad categories of stocks, and then dollar cost average in and never sell.

10. Deciding how you will make a living is one of the most important decisions you will make in life. Look for job availability, an above average salary, and investigate to see if you can expect to be employed your whole working life.

11. Most hobbies, sports, and crafts, have a low probability as a successful, high paying career. Pick a proven career or trade to earn a living, and enjoy the other in your spare time for fun.

12. Owning a debt free place to live in is a key part of your financial goals. Pay off your mortgage as soon as you can, but never interrupt your 20% savings you put away each month.

13. Being frugal is good, being a miser is intolerable. Treat all of your family members with love and acceptance, even if they do not share your goals.

14. Start your wealth building plans as soon as you possibly can. Having a longer time to save means you can build a larger wealth and also have a lower monthly savings goal.

Larry's Recommended Investment Choices

Below are my example of investment choices for a portfolio of ETF's, and also using mutual funds. Both portfolios are broadly diversified, meaning they cover the World, and I also give you a short term bond choice for fixed income in both list. In the mutual fund choices, I have included two funds that emphasize dividends in their stock picking. I like dividends and they help improve long term performance.

You can mix ETF's and mutual funds. In fact, I favor having a mutual fund manager for the International portion of your portfolio. There are other good choices in the market place that you can use instead of the ones I have chosen. Just remember to get the fees down as low as you can.

ETF Portfolio

1. **Large Cap U.S.:** IVV, the iShares Core S&P 500
2. **Small Cap U.S.:** VB, the Vanguard Small Cap ETF.
3. **International:** VEA, the Vanguard FTSE Developed Markets.
4. **Emerging Markets:** IEMG, the iShares MSCI Core Emerging Markets.
5. **Real Estate:** VNQ, the Vanguard REIT ETF.
6. **Short Term Bonds:** VCSH, the Vanguard Short Term Corporate Bond ETF.

Mutual Funds

1. **Large Cap U.S.:** PRDGX – T. Rowe Price Dividend Growth Fund.
2. **Small Cap U.S.:** FCPGX – Fidelity Small Cap Growth Fund.
3. **International:** TRIGX – T. Rowe Price International Growth and Income Fund.
4. **Emerging Markets**: FEMKX – Fidelity Emerging Markets Fund
5. **Real Estate**: FRIFX – Fidelity Real Estate Income Fund
6. **Short Term Bonds**: FSHBX – Fidelity Short Term Bond Fund

Larry's Reading List

I have listed the books that helped me with my plans to build net worth. Some of them I have read many times and they still give me inspiration. They are listed in the order that I recommend you read them. Of course, you should see if you can borrow them first at your local library before buying them. I hope they inspire you as well.

1. **The Millionaire Next Door** by Thomas J. Stanley and William D. Danko
    This book, written by two professors, is the results of 20 years of study about the lifestyle, habits, and misconceptions of self-made millionaires. A must read for those trying to amass wealth.

2. **Cashing In On The American Dream, How To Retire At 35**, by Paul Terhourst. Just a great book that is easy to read and inspirational. May be hard to find. He has many good ideas but he retired way too young.

3. **Your Money or Your Life, Transforming Your Relationship With Money and Achieving Financial Independence** by Vicki Robin and Joe Dominguez. They were the first to

publish a detailed plan for tracking and measuring your financial goals.

4. **The Little Book Of Common Sense Investing: The Only Way To Guarantee Your Fair Share Of Stock Market Returns** by John C. Bogle.
The author is the founder of Vanguard Funds and also the creator of index investing. I have often had trouble accepting his advice of investing in index funds and holding forever, but over time, he has proven to be right.

5. **A Wealth of Common Sense. Why simplicity trumps complexity in any investment plan,** by Ben Carlson. There is a lot to learn from this book. First, the author outlines what does not work in investing. He backs up his outline with a ton of statistics and charts. Then he describes how to put together an investment plan that works. Best part is that what does best is also the simplest.

6. **How To Work For A Jerk: Your Success Is The Best Revenge** by Robert Hochheiser. Working for large companies and succeeding is a huge challenge. You are going to need some advice and this book is a great place to start.

7. **The Complete Tightwad Gazette** by Amy Dacyczyn. This is the quintessential book on how to live cheaply. The author had a large family and

still was able to retire early by squeezing all she could out of a dollar.

8. **Mr. Money Mustache** (an internet blog at mrmoneymustache.com). This blog is written by a guy who has followed the path that I recommend. He has great humor and insight into building and managing his wealth. My big disagreement with him is that he retired too early.

9. **How I Turned $1,000 Into Five Million In Real Estate In My Spare Time** by William Nickerson. This book has inspired many people to make a fortune in real estate. Just read the reviews of this book on Amazon. If you do not like investing in the stock market, then this is a powerful and proven alternative way to build wealth.

10. **Simplify Your Life: 100 Ways To Slow Down And Enjoy The Things That Really Matter,** by Elaine St. James. Voluntary Simplicity was a hot topic during the 1990's. There are many books on the subject of simplicity and minimalism besides this one. They are a good source for finding ways to live cheaply.

11. **Ordinary People, Extraordinary Wealth** by Ric Edelman. Ric does his research on personal finance and his advice is very good.

12. **Warren Buffet.** There are many books written about Warren and most are very good. You just cannot go wrong learning from the most successful investor of all time. I recommend reading at least 2 or 3 of them.

About The Author

Larry spent his career working in the transportation lending and leasing business. During his working years, he attained two certifications: Certified Financial Planner, licensee, and Certified Fund Specialist. He no longer holds those certifications. Currently, Larry is happily retired with his wife in Illinois where he enjoys gardening and playing tennis.

www.ingramcontent.com/pod-product-compliance
Lightning Source LLC
Chambersburg PA
CBHW051810170526
45167CB00005B/1954